The Delights of Democracy

The Delights of Democracy

The Triumph of American Politics

Christian P. Potholm

Some of these essays, several under different titles and several in a slightly different form, originally appeared in *The Sun Journal*, except where noted below: "The Delights of Democracy," (Jan. 31, 1999); "Two for One," (Feb. 28, 1999); "The Wild, Wild East," (Mar. 28, 1999); "Up Ye Mighty Francos," (Apr. 25, 1999); "Candidate Positioning," ["Baldacci's Conundrums,"] (May 23, 1999); "Changing Voting Demographics," (June 20, 1999); "In the Abortion Universe," (July 18, 1999); "Free to Be Me," (Aug. 15, 1999); "True in Any Light?," *The Times Record* (Sept. 3–5, 1999); "The Right to Arm Bears?," (Sept. 12, 1999); "Not on the Ballot," (Oct. 10, 1999); "Top Ten," (Nov. 7, 1999); "A Clear and Present Danger," (Dec. 5, 1999); "Millennium Credit," (Jan. 2, 2000); "An Ode to Chuck," (Jan. 30, 2000); "Playing King Lear," (Feb. 27, 2000); "Polling 101," (Mar. 26, 2000); "More Polling Observations," (Apr. 23, 2000); "Gay Rights III," (May 21, 2000); "A Life of Courage," (June 18, 2000); "Gratitude," (July 6, 2000); "Run, Ralphie, Run," (Aug. 13, 2000); "The Kiss," (Sept. 10, 2000); "Campaign Medley," ["A Potpourri of Campaign Wisdom,"] (Oct. 8, 2000); "Arrogance: A Fable," (Nov. 12, 2000); "Strains of Democracy," (Dec. 10, 2000); "Turnout," (Jan. 7, 2001); "For the Common Good," (Feb. 4, 2001); "When a Champion Leaves the Field," (Mar. 3, 2001); "My McKinley," (Mar. 25, 2001); "Democracy Armed," *Bowdoin Forum* (Fall 2001); "A Need for Will" (Oct. 14, 2001).

First Cooper Square Press edition 2002

This hardcover Cooper Square Press edition of *The Delights of Democracy* is an original publication. It is published by arrangement with the author.

Published by Cooper Square Press
A Member of the Rowman & Littlefield Publishing Group
200 Park Avenue South, Suite 1109
New York, New York 10003-1503
www.coopersquarepress.com

Distributed by National Book Network

Library of Congress Cataloging-in-Publication Data
Potholm, Christian P., 1940–
    The delights of democracy / Christian P. Potholm.— 1st Cooper Square Press ed.
    p. cm.
    Includes bibliographical references and index.
    ISBN 0-8154-1216-9 (cloth : alk. paper)
    1. Democracy—United States. 2. Democracy—Maine. I. Title.

JK1726 .P68 2002
320.973—dc21   2002003823

⊗™   The paper used in this publication meets the minimum requirements of
American National Standard for Information Sciences—Permanence of Paper
for Printed Library Materials, ANSI/NISO Z39.48-1992.
Manufactured in the United States of America

To Rex Rhodes, who brought a new drive
and new mission to his paper, his community,
and to my life.

Contents

Introduction

$\mathscr{A}$merica, my America. What a grand country!

At the dawn of the new millennium, we are richer and more powerful than we have ever been since the founding of the Republic in 1776.

Although there have been many attacks on our political system, it remains the envy of most of the world. The election "crisis" of 2000 only underscores how firm and secure is our democracy. Of the world's 160 or so countries, only a few dozen could have the electoral strains we experienced with a virtual tie election and a month of electoral wrangling and confusion as to a winner.

Having been a student of African government for twenty-five years, it became very clear to me just how lucky we were in the early years of our Republic. We had political leaders—Washington, Adams, Jefferson—who put the good of the country first and set a pattern for political behavior which enshrined the democratic principles and processes which are with us today.

Living in Maine, of course, makes it easier to accept such a positive worldview. After all, our state slogan is "Maine, the Way Life Should Be." We believe that.

The Maine political system is open and tolerant. Many voices are heard and appreciated. Individuals and groups can enter the political arena, make themselves heard, and take their ideas to the people. Races are competitive, both for elected offices and in ballot measures. If Republicans and Democrats win most—but not all—major elected offices, they do not control access to the system. Maine's two independent governors, Longley and King, elected in 1974 and 1994, respectively, symbolize the openness of the process to other political philosophies. The Green Party routinely runs candidates for major office. In the 2002 legislative session, with the Maine senate deadlocked, the balance of power was in the hands of an independent state senator, Jill Goldthweight, elected without party affiliation.

I cannot speak for other states or other portions of the political system, but for the Maine major office and ballot measure realms, it is a political system open to talent, ideas, hard work, and good political strategies. Not all political strategies work. Not all are equal in appeal. Not all are as skillfully applied as others. But the openness remains. Citizen participation is high. Voter turnout is among the highest in the nation. Not only is there no crisis in the Maine political system, it is very much a model of openness, civility, honesty, and campaign management.

So when I was asked to write a monthly column for the *Sun Journal*, I quickly accepted and titled it "The Delights of Democracy" since I believe so passionately in those delights and their embodiment in the Maine political system. We have so much to be thankful for and a political system that is open to talent, hard work, and good ideas is a major feature of that worldview.

I am very grateful to the publisher, Rex Rhodes, for the opportunity to write the column—so much that I have dedicated this book to him. Having written a dozen other books and over a hundred articles, I was nevertheless unprepared for the results of writing a column. With books, there is a long lag time between writing something and seeing the public's reaction to it. With scholarly articles, the interval is even longer and the audience of one's peers is often jaded and remote.

Not so with a monthly column in the *Sun Journal*. "The Delights of Democracy" appears in the Sunday edition and by the time I have breakfast that morning, there are usually already e-mails on my computer reacting to its content. This feedback is spirited as well as immediate.

For an author, this is highly rewarding. I would much prefer a negative reaction or disagreement than I would to have no impact. I write the column to educate, but also to provoke controversy and to stimulate public debate. Seeing e-mails (which I think make people less inhibited than letters to the editor) and getting phone messages as well as subsequent letters is highly gratifying.

This is true even when I think the readers have missed the point. Certainly some did when seeing my column, "Gay Rights III." It is included here under the Issues part of the book so interested readers can explore its dimensions for themselves. I thought it to be straightforward and my personal position very clear. I have always been for Gay Rights and in Maine's political history participated along with Will Robinson (media) and Amy Pritchard (campaign manager) in the successful Gay Rights I amendment (the only successful statewide effort thus far).

In indicating my support for Gay Rights, however, I also underscored some of the pitfalls of trying to run a pro-Gay Rights campaign by doing whatever you felt like as opposed to what the people of Maine wanted and the ways polling had to be done on this issue to be accurate. I laid out what needed to be done if Gay Rights were to pass statewide. The resulting campaign turned out to underscore these missed opportunities with uncanny accuracy.

No column of mine before or since has produced such a deluge of comment. Fair enough and I was pleased it did. But the odd thing was that the comments were exactly evenly divided between those people saying I had not read my Bible and asking how could anyone be for such sinful conduct and those saying I was "homophobic"! I continue to take this experience as a powerful lesson: even when we write as clearly as we can, we don't always succeed in being clear to our readers. And—if truth be told—it's also a powerful lesson that not all readers are equal when it comes to comprehending the written word.

One of the unexpected benefits of writing a column is the extent to which the mystic cords of memory bring to consciousness forgotten incidents of childhood or adolescence which have shaped us and which come back into perspective as the political landscape changes. This book is full of these accounts and many people who have commented on the columns indicate that it is these stories which most get and hold their attention. I have chosen for this book some of the columns which generated the most follow up interests and which provide the most enduring insights into the way politics really occurs in the Pine Tree State.

Henry David Thoreau wrote in *Walden*, "A written word is the choicest of relics. It is something at once more intimate with us and more universal than any other work of art. It is the work of art nearest to life itself."[1]

In much the same spirit, I see political writing as an art form, not simply a recitation of what happened and when. And in writing about politics, I am constantly struck by the wisdom of Barry Lopes, here paraphrased: "The political landscape is baffling in its ability to transcend whatever we would make of it."[2] Our analysis, he feels, automatically orders, reorders, and ultimately dissembles and reassembles that landscape. The resulting interior landscape shapes the way others then react to our perceptions of reality.

In trying to grasp and make immediate the essence of the Maine political scene, I have tried to highlight those insights which are at once enduring and which, I believe, capture the ongoing validity of certain aspects as well as perceptions of those aspects.

The book is divided into six sections. Each in turn is designed to cover a particular aspect of democratic politics that I have witnessed.

Part One, Democracy, looks at the essence of democracy as lived in Maine, as well as some of the strains and strengths of the national political system and how these impinge on our lives.

Part Two, Dimensions of Democracy, highlights aspects of the flow of politics and casts into sharp relief some of the processes and aspects of Maine politics as well as some of the behind-the-scenes actors who have influenced its course over the last twenty years. It also focuses on the incredibly pernicious nature of TV censorship, which threatens the very First Amendment values I hold so dear. Nothing I have witnessed in fifty years in politics is potentially so pernicious to the future of electoral democracy in the twenty-first century.

In Part Three, Analyzing Democracy, I have tried to put the basics of Government 101 as applied to the Maine political scene and show a number of ways one can better understand the nature of politics in the twenty-first century. The aim is to give the reader a flavor for the dynamics of candidate and ballot measure campaigns, especially their internal dimensions, as a central purpose of this section.

Political leadership is the focus of Part Four, Leadership in Democracy. All too often we fail to look at the human dimensions of leadership in the polity and see how such dimensions as courage and steadfastness will out and how knavery is, over time, usually punished at the ballot box. Also, the political leaders who have had the biggest impact on the Maine political scene over the last thirty years provide an overarching set of litmus tests with which to compare present and future leaders.

Part Five, Issues in Democracy, is not a guide to a League of Women Voter's debate. Rather it deals with some major issues such as gun control, gay rights, and abortion and the need for candidate positioning in order to be able to deal with that range of issues successfully.

Finally, Part Six, Psychographics and Demographics in Democracy, looks at the basic underpinnings of the Maine political scene and how changes in them—or the lack of change—account for many of the outcomes over the past twenty-five years. Ethnicity and interest groups such as the Sportsman's Alliance of Maine, the Audubon Society, and the Roman Catholic Church appear in the political process with regularity and importance.

I would like to express my appreciation to all those who helped in the preparation of this manuscript.

To Rex Rhodes, who had faith in the project in the beginning and whose tireless efforts have made the *Sun Journal* such a first-class paper and to Mark Mogensen, who always took the extra time to make sure my efforts made sense. And especially to Maria Fuentes, who was so invaluable in the creative process, reading, and improving every single column before it went to press. She is a treasure! David E. Emery, Sandra, Heather, and Erik Dodds Potholm also provided important insights to individual columns. And a special accolade to Patty Ames, who, as my executive assistant, always helps put me in touch with the many "real Maines" and whose insights and startling good humor always brighten up my day and enrich my analysis.

Thanks too for the Bowdoin students in Maine politics who over the years stimulated my thinking so much. Teaching is such a rewarding profession and interaction with students is always stimulating and engaging. I am also very grateful for the research and teaching assistants who helped me out: Travis Cummings, Alice Martin, Jason Fortin, and Megan Savage. As always, Chris Stearns worked especially hard to make my writing clearer and more understandable. A very special thanks to Susan Price, who went above and beyond the call of duty to help me with the final editing process. Her wonderful personality and sharp wit made it all the more enjoyable.

As always, I have enjoyed working with Jed Lyons, publisher of Madison Books, Cooper Square Press, and Rowman & Littlefield and his very able staff, Ross Plotkin and Michael Messina, who did such a great job with the cover, and especially Terry Fischer who supervised production and was so helpful to the process. From Bill Cohen's first Congressional campaign in 1972 to the publication of this book, Jed has been a friend, colleague, and co-conspirator. He continues to have my considerable gratitude.

Harpswell, Maine
Summer 2001

NOTES

1. Henry David Thoreau, *Walden* (New York: Random House, 2000), p. 97.
2. Barry Lopes, *Arctic Dreams* (New York: Charles Scribner's Sons, 1986) p. xxii.

Part I

DEMOCRACY

The Delights of Democracy

Several years ago, Jim Brunelle, the dean of political commentary on Maine Public Television, in reviewing my book *An Insider's Guide to Maine Politics*, was kind enough to charge me with extolling the "delights of democracy."

I plead guilty.

That is just what I have tried to do for the last thirty years in both the classroom and in real life and especially in Maine politics. I have constantly extolled the virtues of our democratic system. And I've been particularly enthusiastic about the ease with which individuals can— with very little effort on their part—have an impact on the public choices we face.

In fact, I tell them Potholm's Axiom 1 is "Our political system is very open to talent."

We in America and we in Maine have so much for which to be thankful. We have a political system, which is open to talent—almost any talent. We in Maine can get involved in politics at almost any level at any time and make our voices heard.

Our political landscape is populated with dozens of people without great wealth or long apprenticeship who have jumped into the Maine political arena and helped to transform it by word and deed. People who left their front yards and their TV sets and went out into the political arena in order to have an impact. People who stopped complaining about our political system long enough to do something about it.

In Maine, there have been dozens of people who went out into the political realm in order to fight for candidates and causes, who initiated ballot measures, or who founded parties or started movements or passed laws, just because they felt there was a need.

People like John Rensenbrink, Maria Fuentes, Bruce Reeves, Tom LaPointe, Joel Abramson, Jim Longley Sr., Georgette Barube, Alan Caron, Mary Adams, Jonathan Carter, George Smith, Pat LaMarche, Brownie Carson, Dave Emery, George Christie, Hal Pachios, Olympia Snowe, Lil Caron, and Kaileigh Tara have made and continue to make Maine political history.

They simply decided to make things happen in the political realm and they have done so. No party bosses appointed them. No big corporations sanctified their efforts. No one insisted on their getting someone's permission.

In recent years, it has not been fashionable to extol the virtues of our democracy or the access we all have to its rich and varied political system. Yet it is there for anyone willing to put even a little time and energy into the effort, anyone willing to sample "the delights of democracy."

However, to do so means one has to cast free from the comfortable and fashionable cynicism of our age, to stop talking about what is wrong and to start trying to do what one thinks is right.

Lost in the torrent of claims as to what is wrong with our political system is the simple fact that very few political systems on the planet are so open to individual initiative.

All it takes is a willingness to go, however briefly, beyond self (although few of those mentioned above left their egos totally at the door!) and risk an effort, not knowing whether you will be rewarded or not—except by your sense of participation for its own sake. But in fact, the vast majority of you will be rewarded, especially in terms of satisfaction.

Political scientists often like to talk of a "polyarchy" in which leaders are chosen by non-leaders as a democratic system. Contrary to what cynics would have us believe, the United States is very much a polyarchy and Maine is more than that; it is a very open polyarchy.

Not only do we non-leaders choose our leaders, we initiate much public policy. Maine is one of several dozen states where citizens can put their causes on the ballot irrespective of what the Legislature wants. Our citizen-generated referenda have to be enacted into law by that body or put out to the people. This means that virtually anybody with a cause who is willing to work hard can get his or her favorite issue on the ballot.

Many say it is too difficult to get on the Maine ballot. They are wrong. It only takes 40,000 signatures of registered voters and virtually any individual and group can do that with a cause. Many others say it is too easy to get on the Maine ballot. They are wrong. It is just right. It is democracy in action in the best possible way on the best possible level, the level of citizen and small group.

Maine's referenda are a clear manifestation of the openness of the political process and show what can be done with even a little initiative. The next time you hear someone bemoaning this law or that law or this or that lack of a law, tell them to get organized, to get off the bench and into the game.

In this book, I hope to show the *hows* and *wherefors* of participation, to highlight some individuals who have made a difference and how they did it.

I also hope to point out how you right now, with no effort on your part, can end up having two votes in each election instead of the one you think you have now.

Yes, that's right, two votes instead of one. I'll indicate how to double your political power with one stroke and, if you listen to me, you will always have two votes instead of one.

I hope also to show how wonderfully open the Maine political system is, to underscore the ease with which ordinary and not-so-ordinary citizens can make a difference in political parties, in campaigns, in causes, and especially in ballot measures of which Maine has three or four or five almost every year.

It has never been easier to participate in Maine politics on all levels. I hope you will join me on this journey to the delights of democracy.

Strains of Democracy

*W*inston Churchill was fond of comparing democracy to a raft in contrast with the ship of monarchy. Monarchy, he said, sailed along like a glorious clipper ship until it hit a rock and then it sank. With democracy, it was messy and your feet were always wet but it didn't sink even when it hit obstacles.

This analogy may be small comfort as we examine the aftermath of the presidential election of 2000. The deluge of lawsuits, partisan bickering, talking head pontificating, and the seeming endless cycle of charge and countercharge has left many with election fatigue and democratic upset.

There has been so much to dislike that it is hard to know where to begin. Still, an attempt can be made. For me, it started off election night. I had reconciled myself to a Gore victory and when the networks called it that way early, I went off to concentrate on the Maine election ballot where questions one, two, and three had occupied most of my attention during the campaign.

But my irritation was considerable when Tom Brokaw referred to Gore's win as "our victory," and it became clear the networks (by default if not design) had called Florida even before the polls in the western, more Republican part of the state had even voted. How difficult is it to do exit polling in two different time zones? It was worth the price of admission however, later to watch the look on Katie Couric's face when Florida was taken out of the Gore column. She looked like she'd swallowed a toad! Then the networks lurched in the other direction, calling the state more than a little prematurely, for Bush.

But election night was nothing compared to the fiascoes that followed. First you had Jessie Jackson and what one commentator called his "rent-a-riot." Then you had crazed ladies of Palm Beach county getting all excited because they had spoiled 19,000 ballots this time compared to the 15,000 they'd spoiled the last time around. None of those interviewed looked too shy to ask the clerk for a new ballot in any case! Later, Republican stalwarts chanted "stop the count, stop the count" and Miami/Dade election officials did just that. Watching all this, you had to have some admiration for the Founding Fathers and their idea of the Electoral College to put election results at arm's length from these types of street demonstrations.

And so it went, with men and women behaving badly and Republican partisans trying to catch up to the Democrats in terms of wild claims and dubious behavior as plane loads of lawyers (including Maine's very own Tony Buxton) jetted in to "sort things out." It's been a circus.

But what relevance for democratic theory and practice?

First, we need to pay attention only to people who are consistent. If you liked the Electoral College when it looked like Gore was going to win it but lose the popular vote, you have to still like it. Vice versa for the Bush supporters. Also, the old adage "Where you stand depends on where you sit" applied to the many partisans on both sides who saw diametrically opposite implications for the same action.

Second, just because one doesn't like the outcome of this particular election cycle is no reason to scrap a system that has worked for a couple of hundred years with only an occasional problem. Keep the Electoral College.

Third, this whole process underscores for me, the real power of our system. In many other parts of the world, the political systems are so fragile that the military would have stepped in that first morning after people took to the streets and taken over the political system.

Fourth, I have been saying for eight years that Clinton is the first president I know who loved political campaigns so much he turned his two terms as president into one perpetual campaign and never gave up the fight. Remember, this is a chap who on the day he was impeached held a pep rally on the White House lawn and got away with it. Gore clearly adopted this stance as well. I saw him four weeks after the election was over declaring "I'm going to win this election" as if it were still going on!

Fifth, the election results show very clearly how divided the nation is in terms of ideology. Neither the right nor the left can claim a mandate. The center holds. Why is that bad? Also, I think Clinton was such a dominant player on the scene, striding across the TV always campaigning that he simply overshadowed both Gore and Bush and I have no doubt if he could have run for a third term he would have won handily.

Sixth, neither candidate has covered himself with glory in the post-election period. Bush often looked like a deer in the headlights, off-kilter, bewildered, and unsure. Gore and especially Joe Lieberman's lugubrious and unctuous self-righteousness was very grating as they called for "counting" ballots which had already been counted twice, albeit not the way they wanted them counted with one Republican and one Democratic counter and a Democratic supervisor to decide each individual ballot! For his part, poor Dick Cheney, wounded and tired and bedridden looked like he really wished he were back in the less stressful oil service business.

Yet it will all come out well in the end. The lawyers will be sent home—or at least people will stop paying them $300 an hour to make trouble, not solve problems. Various cities and towns will decide to update voting procedures and methods. And the losing partisans will start up the 2004 campaign while all voters and non-voters will have been given a lesson in citizenship that every vote does count (unless, of course, it is "chadded"). The stock market will rise again once the Federal Reserve cuts interest rates again. The economy will run its own course, hopefully aided by a divided government.

Right now, our feet are cold and wet, we are tired and frustrated at the slow pace of our raft and we keep bumping into more lawyer-rocks than we ever have imagined. But no thanks to the overwrought partisans on both sides, democracy will win out.

Democracy will win out.

That's the real lesson of this turbulent and seemingly unending election ride.

POSTSCRIPT

As Americans, we can all be proud of the way the American political system performed during the 2000 election cycle. The aftermath of the closest election in American history was messy and agonizing, but safely done. Power was peacefully passed from one party to another, even though many in the second had significant doubts about the fairness of the election. The good of the total political system won out over partisan beliefs and efforts.

Democracy Armed

$\mathscr{F}$or Maine political figures, defense-related issues have always been important. In fact, for the last fifty years of Maine politics, support for a strong national defense has been one of the bedrock, core values for the political culture. Defense-related facilities and their future are woven into the fabric and mystique of Maine politics. And this is as it should be for the state that sent the highest per capita number of its citizens to fight in the American Civil War.

Continuing support for the defense industry and bases has traditionally cut across party and ideological lines. Conservative Republicans and liberal Democrats and virtually all ideological hues in between have consistently supported such defense-related activities as the Brunswick Naval Air Station, the Bath Iron Works (BIW), the Kittery Naval Shipyard, Saco Defense, and Loring Air Force base. When Margaret Chase Smith was the ranking Republican on the Senate Armed Services and Appropriations committees, Maine even had Strategic Air Command bases in Bangor and Presque Isle. Senators Ed Muskie and George Mitchell took a backseat to no one in promoting Loring or BIW.

Occasionally, political figures have taken a different position. In 1993, for example, Congressman Tom Andrews departed from the position of the Maine Congressional delegation and suggested that Loring Air Force Base be closed as unnecessary. He was subsequently punished for that deviation when he ran against Congresswoman Olympia Snowe for the U.S. Senate in 1994. She won by a larger than expected margin of 60 percent to 34 percent (with Independent candidate Plato Truman getting 3.4 percent of the vote). She carried normally Democratic Aroostok County (where the base was located) by an impressive margin of 71.8 percent to 24.4 percent over Andrews and 3.8 percent for Truman. Even though Andrews late could well feel vindicated because Loring was eventually closed during the very next round of national base closings, his refusal to support the defense agenda of the state cost him dearly. He may have been "right" on the issue but he was out of step with the people of Maine.

In this chapter, we seek to place the Maine concerns over national defense within a broader national and historical context. Over a hundred years ago, Carl von Clausewitz wrote:

> The fact that slaughter is a horrifying spectacle must make us all take war more seriously, but not provide an excuse for gradually blunting our swords in the name of humanity. Sooner or later someone will come along with a sharp sword and hack off our arms."[1]

More than a hundred years after the posthumous publication of his seminal work, *On War*, Carl von Clausewitz remains the premier authority on the nature of war and especially the relationship between politics and war. As we in America look toward a new administration in this new century, it is useful to examine that relationship anew, especially in light of Clausewitz's impact on both the military establishment and some incoming members of the new administration, most notably Colin Powell.

For Clausewitz, war is a continuation of politics by other means. It is not an aberration, not something "inhuman," but rather something very human, almost commonplace, and very much connected to the political life of states. War, he feels, should always be subordinated to policy but it cannot either be ignored or wished away. This inner connection between war and politics is most helpful in seeing how to avoid war while preserving core national interests.

He also captures the critical essence of war, that clash of the powerful duality "I want—You want." War is thus a clash of wills: "an act of force to compel our enemy to do our will." By going to the very heart of war and seeing it so clearly, Clausewitz helps us to dispense with so many extra aspects and to focus on the essence of conflict.

For Clausewitz, while going to war is something to be avoided if possible, once committed to war, all necessary force should be used:

> Kind-hearted people might of course think there was some ingenious way to disarm or defeat an enemy without too much bloodshed, and might imagine this is the true goal of the art of war. Pleasant as it sounds, it is a fallacy that must be exposed: war is such a dangerous business that the mistakes that come from kindness are the very worst."[2]

War, he says, is simply so terrible that we must get it over with as quickly as possible.

This perspective is embedded at the heart of the Powell Doctrine, the current Pentagon military action philosophy named for General Colin Powell who, as head of Joint Chiefs of Staff, articulated the doctrine to be applied before U.S. military forces were used. This doctrine includes three major elements:

1. Establish clearly defined and achievable objectives right at the outset.
2. *Apply overwhelming force quickly.*
3. Establish a completed exit strategy in place before the engagement begins.

With Colin Powell as American Secretary of State, both the doctrine and Clausewitz's underlying set of assumptions will be very much back in vogue. Interestingly enough, I have never found Clausewitz to be simply "that bloody Prussian." He warns most persuasively about the power of war to get out of hand. He believes war acquires its own momentum, which operates independent of political logic and rational cost-benefit calculations. The god of War, Mars, has his own imperatives.

For decades in this century, the principle decision makers in the United States resisted these notions and tried to calibrate the United States to other circumstances, other "realities" such as Woodrow Wilson's "war to end all wars." Yet this century has shown the folly of pretending that any war is the "last" war.

Whether we call the tendency "an arms race" or something else, there is a momentum to the procurement of weapons among states and indeed the weapons acquisition process becomes a kind of communication among states. True peace cannot come from unilateral disarmament or unilateral weapons freezes.

Sun Tzu wrote "Warfare is the greatest affair of state, the basis of life and death, the Tao to survival or extinction. It must be thoroughly pondered and analyzed."[3] Yet while few would disagree with the import of this statement, one of the most difficult aspects of a functioning democracy is the extent to which the scarce resources of the polity should be devoted to the study of, and preparation for, the defense of the state.

> How much of the national treasure should be allocated to defense
>   and war making?
> How to prepare for war in times of peace?
> What historical model should be followed?

There are two major strands in Western military theory and practice. The first, typified by the approach developed by some of the early Greek city-states, revolves around intermittent warfare and the preparation for warfare. The polity faces a threat. Political decision makers decide to react to the threat. Yeomen farmers drop their agricultural implements and pick up their weapons and go off to fight.

In this model, encounters are short, sharp, and decisive and wars are often of limited duration. Once the threat is passed, the "army" is disbanded and the farmers go back to farming. This citizen-based army was both idealized in Western military thought and criticized as the state comes to face different and more ongoing challenges.

Another strand is often identified with the transition in the Roman polity from Republic to Empire where the citizen-based, stop and go form of military activity eventually gave way to the adoption of a larger, permanent standing army. This permanent army was on continuous duty, available for defense and, as things turned out, offensive activities as the polity expanded. It also turned out to have disastrous implications for the political system as the legions became the instruments for ongoing military interference in the political life of the state.

Much of American history shows an oscillation between these two models. Major crises, such as the American Civil War, World War I, and World War II, have produced massive expansion of the armed forces and a huge commitment of scarce resources to the endeavor. A national draft was instituted for all three wars and there was a vast, even explosive growth in the size of the "professional" armed forces.

But once the war was over, there followed a very rapid reduction in the size of the forces, a concomitant shrinking of the professional core, and an unwillingness to pay for weapons systems upgrades without a perceived threat. A unilateral disarmament strategy prevailed.

In reality, we must recognize that two things can be true simultaneously and that the United States is heir to both traditions. Assumptions embedded in both models come to influence our views on military matters, providing the 280 million Americans with a wide spectrum of beliefs about what model can—or should—be followed.

For those who have grown up living in the United States since the advent of the Cold War, it is very difficult to even imagine the pattern that prevailed prior to that situation so that some historical background is necessary.

The United States ended World War II with thirteen million men and women in the armed forces, the largest navy in the history of the world, and a huge air force as well as a nuclear monopoly.

But within a matter of months, the United States had disarmed itself to the point of abject military poverty. In fact, when the Korean War broke out in June 1950, that poverty was cast in sharp relief when the United States tried to enter the conflict with authority.

Ordered by President Truman to stop North Korean aggression against South Korea, the American commander in the Far East, General Douglas MacArthur, hastily cobbled together a small ad hoc force drawn from the 24th division in Japan under the direction of Colonel Charles (Brad) Smith. Members of this small force had never trained together. Few had any combat training, let along experience. The unit lacked artillery. They had no tanks. Their anti-tank weapons were hopelessly out of date. Their radios did not work. Their rations were leftovers from World War II and inedible. Rushed to Korea, the force was soon destroyed by the North Koreans.

"Task Force Smith" became a metaphor for military unpreparedness and even today, in the halls of the Pentagon, "Remember Task Force Smith" still echoes as a warning against a failure to anticipate military needs. Coupled with the more generalized historical trauma of the Japanese attack on Pearl Harbor, it serves as a powerful impetus to keep the American military going, causing those charged with military responsibility to say "Never again."

The Korean War also cast in sharp relief the global limits of U.S. power under any realistic set of circumstances. When MacArthur ordered his ill-fated lunge toward the Chinese/Korean border of the Yalu River, he used one marine and six American army divisions. At that time, the United States only had eleven divisions in its entire army. Leaving aside the fact that the Chinese had over 250 divisions, the use of two-thirds of all U.S. ground forces in the world in one location, far from their bases in a dubious and ill-advised mission, indicated how unprepared the United States was for global force projection.

Yet, it is from this era of the 1950s, that the American military conceived of the two wars doctrine, that the United States should always be prepared to fight one major and one minor war *at the same time*. However unrealistic this approach might be in practice, it does suggest that from that point on, American military doctrine clearly had chosen the Roman standing army model over the Greek citizen-soldier model. It remains the basis for much military planning today even though 2001 saw the doctrine debated even more forcefully than previously.

But adopting the model of the garrison state, the polity perpetually armed and devoting an ongoing percentage of its gross domestic product to preparation for war has not settled the questions about the degree of preparation necessary.

For the last fifty years, the American polity has constantly questioned both the size of the military and the percentage of national treasure devoted to the military on an annual budget, which has formed much of the national debate. How much is enough? What weapon systems are necessary? What are the most cost-effective procurement procedures? What is the proper balance between pay for members of the armed forces, money spent on training versus weapons, indeed which weapons systems provide the best protection for which portion of which branch of the service?

It is thus the yearly fluctuations and the applications of that holistic military enterprise which have concerned the American public and its leaders during the Cold War and its immediate aftermath.

Embedded in that history of democracy armed were two other seminal events, neither of which turned out as expected. The long and torturous Vietnam War (1965–1975) ended with the United States defeated, the morale of its armed forces at an extremely low ebb, and its military cupboards bare. The Gulf War (1991), however, left the United States globally supreme, having won the most one-sided war in modern times with fewer casualties than could be normally expected during a year of peace! If everything had gone wrong in Vietnam, everything went right in the Gulf. Yet few realize that many of the reforms in military doctrine as well as training and weapons systems which shone so brightly in the Gulf War were actually products of the bitter Vietnam experiences.

But beyond the size of the armed forces, the limits of force projection, differences of approach to various weapons systems, and the relative strength of the United States versus its potential adversaries lie some more fundamental questions as to what keeps the international peace and how the United States in this new century can maximize the likelihood of both continued hegemony and peace.

These are two different but obviously related issues of note:

What forces lead to hegemony?
What ingredients keep the peace?

Politicians, statesmen, scholars, and warriors have long debated these questions and the entire body of literature would take several book-length forays to cover. But several scholars are persuasive to me in their arguments that military preparedness lies at the heart of deterrence.

Donald Kagan, for example, in his *On the Origins of War and the Preservation of Peace*, points to the "grave dangers of complacency and unpreparedness," arguing that it is not simply a matter of arms and armies but of will, the will to prepare for war in order to preserve the peace.[4]

For his part, John Stoessinger sees misperceptions, particularly a leader's misperception of his adversary's power, as the "quintessential cause of war" and of what he terms "war lovers" men such as Saddam Hussein or Adolph Hitler "who will not stop unless they are stopped."[5]

Yet some are uncomfortable with the notion of the United States as hegemonic, as the world's peacekeeper and preserver of the status quo. Others wonder how to reconcile the America of democracy with hegemonic America? How to be prudent in taking American responsibility for world peace and stability?

The United States has a unique and vital role in the world order today and, for good or for evil, that role is huge and filled with a variety of responsibilities. The United States is globally hegemonic with peacekeeping functions in Asia as well as Europe. Would China invade Taiwan without the 7th Fleet to prevent them? Would North Korea venture south without the U.S. 3rd division in South Korea as a "trip wire?" Would NATO exist, let alone function without U.S. participation and leadership? Could the Balkans have been stabilized without the massive initiative and presence of U.S. troops?

Critics of the role of the United States as hegemonic, I suggest, would be hard pressed to come up with better and more positive alternatives to the United States as peacekeeper. Simply put, who would do a better job at keeping the peace and pushing the values of democracy and stable global commerce?

For its role as a hegemonic power, the United States fits very comfortably in the overarching tradition of Western military supremacy and global activity.

Geoffrey Parker in his somewhat overlooked but profound work on military and political interaction, sees five critical elements which have played such important roles in the history of the West. In fact, he links the global rise of the West to its relationship with the ongoing art of war.[6]

Parker postulates that the societies of the West have proven particularly adroit at waging war and have made it a central state activity since the time of the Greeks and the Romans. But it is the states of the West in the post–1648 Treaty of Westphalia world which have been most willing to dedicate so much more of their scarce resources to war craft for a longer period of time than their competitors elsewhere in the world.

For Parker, these key ingredients are: (1) an accent on superior technology, (2) superior discipline, (3) an aggressive military tradition, (4) receptivity to innovation, and (5) an ability and willingness to finance continual arms races.

To these I would add a very important additional factor, the belief that there will always be another war. That is, there must be the assumption that there will be another war so that you have to prepare for war in times of peace. This, it seems to me, is central to an ongoing interest in upgrading weapons and military personnel.

While Parker is describing the longer term traditions of the Western way of war, and is principally concerned with the global expansion of the West (from controlling 13 percent of the world's surface to controlling 85 percent of it), there is a striking, almost eerie quality to those characteristics when approaching American military preeminence.

The United States almost perfectly fits Parker's paradigm for success in this cultural and historical context.

The United States is foremost in the world in terms of military technology and determined to remain so. Its armed forces are based on the notion of superior training for an all-volunteer force. The United States displays an aggressive military ethos, not in terms of foreign adventures but "aggressive" in terms of integrating new weapons systems and absorbing military technology as fast as it can be generated.

This capacity to accept innovation stands in stunning contrast to the rest of the world's military establishments who have neither the luxury of new weapons systems on such a regular basis nor the military tradition of accepting them. But the feature that distinguishes the United States most prominently is the fifth, the willingness to pay for military innovation. This willingness to constantly explore new weapons systems is the hallmark of military success and its guarantor. We must always keep this in mind when considering what we as a society feels is important enough to do in any given budget cycle.

This is not to say there is no waste in military procurement. This is not to say there are no redundant weapons systems. This is not to say we don't need all the hardware innovations. But the trick is to know when to stop. It is infinitely better to have too much than too little. Reagan may have almost bankrupted the United States combining his tax cuts with military expansion, but he did bankrupt the Soviet Union. Current discussions about the building of a light missile shield need to be placed in that context, cost benefit ratios.

Parker's analysis of force projection is particularly relevant to America's present hegemonic status.[7] He points out the extent to which the maritime countries of the West married the new technology of the cannon to newly designed ships and were thus able to project their force around the globe and gain world domination. Coupled with new tactics which advocated standing off and firing at enemy ships rather than grappling with them in hand-to-hand combat, the navies of the Western countries defeated their adversaries over and over again.

Sea power was thus the most important revolution in terms of European force projection.[8] Times have changed, aircraft carrier battle groups have replaced ships of the line but the principle remains the same: force projection requires advanced technology, great expense, and constant training.

The carrier battle groups of the United States are the direct descendants of the armed sailing ships both in terms of tactics (stand off and deliver force from afar) and in the process of projecting an individual country's power across the globe. In lieu of many forward bases, American power is projected into Asia and Africa and the Mediterranean and the Gulf region. If foreign conquest is no longer the goal, keeping the global peace and the economic system it underpins are vital to the maintenance of American values and supremacy as well as to world peace.

But advanced military technology and the ability to project force across the globe in order to protect basic national interests are not enough to insure success in warfare. Clausewitz remains the premier authority on the nature of war *qua* war. His emphasis on small unit cohesion as the basis for the success of military operations and the need for constant training lies at the heart of military preparedness. Only intensive training and tight small unit cohesion can overcome what he so aptly termed "the friction of war."

Morale, training, experience, a sense of honor and duty, discipline, and loyalty all must be instilled over and over until the units in battle can perform their duties in spite of the friction which has no parallel in other aspects of human endeavor.

Wherever one comes down on the ongoing series of debates about military procurement, new weapons, military pay, methods of recruitment, and indeed the limits of American power, one must always deal with the bedrock demands of training, discipline, and commitment to new military technology if the United States is to remain hegemonic. We can all disagree about what the hegemonic United States should do but it is hard to imagine the world a better place with the United States replaced as hegemonic.

How then to balance "national" interests, especially national security issues with other demands such a stopping ethnic cleansing or genocide? How far ahead should one plan? What about a missile defense, not against the major nuclear power Russia, but the smaller North Korea, Iran, or Iraq? Resolving this dilemma lies beyond the scope of this chapter but its resolution must take place within the matrix of the conflicting aspects of American military history and doctrine, the place of the democracy armed. How to balance the needs of fulfilling our peacekeeping commitment and increasing our military readiness? At the dawn of the twenty-first century, we must do both but how?

In the last analysis, these are not easy questions to answer and, indeed, some may be unanswerable. But in order to begin to understand the questions themselves, it is necessary to see the United States embedded in the realities of both existing war craft and the difficulties in understanding the bases for future activity.

The dictates of Mars, the god of war, are always with us, not just in the past but in the future as well. There will always be another war. The implications of this assertion may be unpleasant but necessary to avoid being unprepared for the next calamity. Legitimate questions must be asked as a new administration arrives.

Currently, the United States spends 3.4 percent of our gross domestic product on defense. This is the lowest percentage of our gross domestic product devoted to defense since before Pearl Harbor! Over the past decade, the American military has been asked to roughly triple its overseas deployment as commitments have risen sharply in such areas as the Balkans. At the same time, America's armed forces have shrunk by approximately 40 percent since the Gulf War.

The next administration needs to examine all of our current commitments and our need to upgrade both weapons systems and training activities to improve readiness all across the military spectrum. Remember that it takes $1.5 billion a year to maintain a single carrier battle group (an aircraft carrier, submarines, guided missile cruisers, and frigates plus support ships) every year.

With a battle group currently required in each of the Indian Ocean/Gulf region, the Mediterranean, and the Pacific, one needs at least three carrier battle groups in operation (including resupply, rotation, and maintenance) for each one on station. There is a huge cost involved just in keeping even with current demands. A single aircraft carrier and one hundred planes for it costs two-thirds the total of Great Britain's entire defense budget. Only the United States can afford to pay the price of being hegemonic in today's global military configurations.

Whenever I go to Washington, I try to revisit two national memorials. The Vietnam memorial never fails to move me. Its massive power suggests the magnitude of the horror of war as well as the shining points of individual sacrifice and courage. But it is not the monument *qua* monument that impacts me as much as the interaction between the people who visit the monument and the monument. The veterans and their families playing out the individual dramas of loss and remembrance; the flowers, medals, combat badges all left as at a shrine of great holiness; these combine again and again to impact the onlooker.

But the Korean memorial stirs me even more. The Ghost Patrol is there, forever marching to their doom. You do not need people around to get its full impact. You do not need the interaction that is such a part of the Vietnam memorial. You simply stand there and watch it, overcome by that sense of doom.

You do not know whether that doom that is coming is coming in the next millisecond or minute or hour or day but the doom is there. The patrol will not survive. There is, of course, inevitable doom in real war. And we, the survivors and beneficiaries, must always accept the horror of that aspect of war.

In a democracy and knowing that cost of war, we must try never to make war without firm purpose with higher goals than territory or power or resources. We must always seek peaceful alternatives where they exist, knowing that in some times and some places there are no peaceful alternatives.

While at peace, we hate to think of that doom ever occurring again, the sacrifices in blood and treasure and the hopes of young and old.

But we know in our hearts and our minds that war will come again. And our degree of preparedness affects both the likelihood of success and the likelihood of avoidance. We owe it to all the patrols of the future.

As the Korean memorial says so cogently, "Freedom is not free."

For a free people, the price of freedom is always there and must be paid, either now or later. Only democracy armed—well armed and trained well—can keep the peace. Or make winning the next war more likely.

NOTES

1. Carl von Clausewitz, *On War* (New York: Knopf, 1993), p. 309.

2. von Clausewitz, *On War* (New York: Borzoi Books, 1993), pp. 83–84.

3. Sun-Tzu and Sun Pin, *The Complete Art of War,* translation and commentary by Ralph D. Sawyer with the collaboration of Mei-chun Lee Sawyer (Boulder: Westview Press, 1996), p. 40.

4. Donald Kagan, *On the Origins of War and the Preservation of Peace* (New York: Doubleday, 1995).

5. John Stoessinger, *Why Nations Go to War* (Boston: St. Martin's, 2001), pp. 258, 260.

6. See Geoffrey Parker "The Western Way of War" in Geoffrey Parker, ed., *The Cambridge Illustrated History of Warfare* (Cambridge: University of Cambridge Press, 1995), pp. 2–9.

7. See Geoffrey Parker, *The Military Revolution* (Cambridge: Cambridge University Press, 1988).

8. Interestingly enough, Peter Padfield sees a strong correlation between maritime supremacy and the rise of capitalism and democracy. See Peter Padfield, *Maritime Supremacy and the Opening of the Western Mind* (New York: The Overlook Press, 2000).

For the Common Good

$\mathscr{P}$resident Bush's 2001 inaugural address accented our commonality and our need for unity of purpose to make America a better place. In an odd sort of way, the very closeness of the presidential race has cast in sharp relief the racial and cultural divides we as a nation face.

You couldn't tell from the Maine election results where Al Gore not only won the state handily, he carried many of the rural areas (in Aroostock and Washington counties) as well as the principal urban areas of Lewiston, Portland, and Bangor. But for the rest of the country there was a breathtakingly sharp division with the Republican candidate carrying most of the rural counties all over the country and the Democratic candidate carrying most of the urban counties nationwide.

Obviously larded into this split is the troubling aspect of race. Despite getting 27 percent of the African American vote in Texas in his last gubernatorial race, Bush only garnered 9 percent of that vote nationally. In part, this was due to African American assumptions about the Republican Party and its values, and its "true" attitudes toward inclusion. The party of Abraham Lincoln currently simply does not signal racial inclusion to most African Americans.

It was also due to the demonizing of Bush and his values, both by Democrats and many black leaders. The director of the NAACP is Kweise Mfume, a former Democratic Congressman. In this cycle, the NAACP ran one of the most hurtful and deceptive ads, linking the dragging death of an African American man to the Texas of George W. Bush!

Ironically, of course, the two white men who committed this most hateful murder had already been convicted by a Texas court and await execution for the murder. And we know that in George W.'s Texas, executions for murder take place.

Sadly, there was once a time when the NAACP stood for the very best values of inclusion and community.

There was also a time when many more Americans had the hope that the racial divide in our country could be bridged. In the sixties, I remember standing with others, black and white, holding hands and singing "We Shall Overcome" in protest to the visit to Harvard of George Wallace. While society was still segregated, our hearts were not. And we felt that in the future, the promise of racial equality and justice would be reached.

I went on to do my Ph.D. research in Africa and again, there the 1960s were a time of great hope. Independence would bring African countries to their rightful place in the world order; African leaders would right the wrongs of colonialism and bring advancement for the peoples of that continent. And that in turn, along with learning about their rich and powerful heritage would encourage African Americans to move forward in American society.

First at Dartmouth and later at Vassar, I was privileged to be chosen by the black students to be their advisor for the Afro-American society even though there were already African American professors on campus. This was, I think, due in part to both my knowledge of, and experience in, Africa. Having lived all of my life in a society that was 90 percent white and then in one which was 90 percent black could not help but lead me to the conclusion that the "common good" in any society must include everyone's good.

While at Dartmouth, I met two black students, Tiny and Henry. They were gang leaders from Chicago who had been recruited by Dartmouth in a very stretching outreach effort. They were tough, streetwise guys who were part of the Mayor Daley machine, still on the payroll for keeping things quiet and they would often fly back to Chicago for "consultations."

They were also interested in guns and since I was always looking for hunting partners in those days, we were soon festooned with bandoleers of ammunition and wandering about in the woods of New Hampshire and Vermont. I must confess it was worth the price of admission to watch the expressions on people's faces when the three of us came out of the woods and into the general store for lunch. Armed black men were a rare sight in rural Vermont, I can tell you that.

But these guys didn't turn out to be very good hunters. They never killed any game, despite being very good shots. Tiny, in particular, had a soft spot for animals. "Chris, how is the mother squirrel going to explain to the baby squirrels you just killed their father?" Having these guys in class was a joy. They were intrigued with learning and self-confident enough to dive in with a million questions. "This beats the streets by a mile," said Henry as he applied for his junior year in France.

They were positive influences on the student body, both black and white. I remember they tried to tell the other students that rhetoric could only get you so far, that you wanted people "competing" for your support, not taking it for granted. They always challenged us to see if problems could be solved, not tensions continued. They also cautioned me about using phrases such as "speaking as an African American"!

Henry and Tiny were courageous and true to their beliefs and acted on them even when their moderate views were unpopular. The night Martin Luther King Jr. was killed, Tiny called me and said "The [expletive deleted] want to burn down the library. You'd better get over here." "I think telling them not to would mean a lot more coming from you and Henry" I replied and the Dartmouth library was not torched that horrible and tragic night.

It would, of course, be very wrong and hypocritically judgmental to blame black leadership for the racial divide in America today. In my view, African Americans are justified in holding many of their views about white America. There are still too many Americans who simply will not accept them as equals no matter what they do or how they act.

But—and it's a big but—this country needs bold and brave and daring African American leaders to reach out and try to work with all those who would close that divide no matter what their party or background. I have always thought it made no sense at all for African Americans to get so caught up in the rhetoric of the Democratic Party and the ideology of white liberals that they lost the political leverage a true swing voting group can have—as well as the diversity of ideas necessary to combat racism on all levels. By contrast, many Asian

Americans and Hispanics seem to understand this and make their votes count for more in the calculations of both parties.

There are undoubtedly some Republicans in Congress who could give a fig about black aspirations. Would, in fact, start a second Marcus Garvey "Back to Africa" movement if they could. Who rejoice every time a black leader such as Jessie Jackson stumbles.

But, why strengthen the hand of these individuals by snubbing George Bush as President? When the Black Caucus walked out on Bush's certification they made a point they undoubtedly believed in. But did that gesture really move the racial situation along in a positive direction? And to have Jessie Jackson Jr. do the walk out three times for the TV cameras hardly seemed a positive step of "inclusion."

We all need hope again. We need men and women of goodwill who will rededicate themselves to the struggle for equality and for the responsibility of the common good. Racism is not in the common good.

I say all of America and especially minorities should take George Bush at face value and put him in the position of doing what he says he wants to do, heal the racial and cultural divides we face. If he doesn't perform, fine, punish him in 2004 at the ballot box; but until then, don't make a self-fulfilling prophecy out of things by rejecting his statements out of hand. We do not need self-fulfilling prophecies of non-cooperation.

For the common good, we need dedicated leaders at all levels and from all groups of society reaching out to one another to actualize the promise that still is America.

I want to believe him when President Bush said: " I will work to build a single nation of justice and opportunity."

I want others to as well. To heal the racial divide that still exists so hurtfully in 2001 America, we need the efforts of all people of good-will.

It is our challenge as well as his.

A Need for Will

$\mathcal{L}$ast Saturday, my daughter got married in Boothbay Harbor. It was a grand weekend and a lovely time. On Friday, with some free time, I drove around Lincoln and Knox counties enjoying a glorious Indian summer day. I'm always intrigued by the way Maine communities take shape and I especially like to visit the harbors—such as East Boothbay, South Bristol, or New Harbor—which combine working waterfronts with pleasure boats in almost equal measure: blue collar and Yuppie blended together as the whole state of Maine is now.

But this excursion was different. It was the flags and the home-made signs. I must have seen 5,000 American flags, on trailers and mansions, on country stores and wharves. Flags everywhere. And signs: "United We Stand," "America the Proud," "Together We Will Triumph," "All Pull Together," "God Bless America." In my entire life, I've never seen anything like this display of real patriotism and solidarity.

And yet, there was a poignancy to this outpouring of American spirit. It wasn't just that everything is diffused with grief for the tragedies in New York City and Washington and Pennsylvania; it was a palpable loss of innocence and security. I'll always remember the elderly lady at Pemaquid Point lighthouse who explained wistfully, "I hope they don't come and blow up our lighthouse." We're all anxious now, waiting for the next act of terror, and we all personalize our own fears and project them onto the trip we were going to take or the plane ride we have to go on or the water supply or the nuclear power plant or whatever. The terrorists have hijacked our innocence.

35

For that's what it was—innocence. It wasn't just the fact that the action took place on American soil and in American airspace, although that has happened often in our history. It's the magnitude. Again, not just the visual impact, but because the casualty list is so staggering. In terms of causalities, the World Trade Center bombing is far worse than Pearl Harbor, as bad as Iwo Jima, Okinawa, or Antietam—the bloodiest day in American history. It is a grim and tragic legacy of twenty-first century terror.

This is a free county and we have to cherish the very values that now allow—even demand—some of our fellow citizens and others to excuse the terrorist attacks by citing inhumanity to Palestinians, or American hegemony (as if any other major power would be better for global peace), or portraying the mujahideen as "freedom fighters."

We can, however, be excused from accepting any of this foolishness. These are not freedom fighters but psychopathic killers who deserve to be exterminated and if they wish to go directly to paradise, we should assist them in any way we can. There is no need for us to accompany them or to even give them the opportunity to go on that journey to paradise at our expense.

In his monumental work, *On War*, Karl von Clausewitz probes into the nature of war more clearly and deeply than any other military analysis I have ever read. At base, he says, war is simply a contest of wills. You win wars when you break your opponent's will. Nothing else matters.

We must never forget that the terrorists base their actions on the supposition that their will is stronger than our own. That, as a people, we Americans make war now only if it can be very short and very bloodless. After all, we won the last war in Kosovo without a single combat death and whether in Lebanon or Somalia, we often get involved where we shouldn't, and, after suffering casualties, withdraw. We have seldom followed up in a sustained fashion attacks and probes of our will such as the bombing of the USS Cole or the destruction of the American embassies in Nairobi and Dar es Salaam.

We are an impatient people, accustomed to incredible riches and near perfect security and spoiled by more than 150 years without foreign invasion. That is what the terrorists count on.

We must have the will to see those thousands avenged and the perpetrators exterminated. "Bringing them to justice" has a nice, law-abiding sound to it. But this truly is war and these murderers are beyond the law as we know it. They are utterly contemptuous of it and us. They call us "crusaders," and by that they mean the Christian crusaders from the eleventh and twelfth centuries! They hate with such primordial feeling that they sign suicide notes and then are content not to act on those notes for five years. They want nothing but the destruction of us and our way of life. There can never be a successful accommodation with those who wish to destroy us. A Palestinian homeland and a lifting of sanctions against Iraq are but false banners under which they are clever enough to operate.

We must have the patience to see this war won if it takes five months or five years or five decades. There are many enemy "centers of gravity" as Clausewitz would say and it will take a great deal of time and a major effort to root them out and destroy them all. We must have the will for a sustained campaign, else we shall fail and those thousands of people will have died in vain. And the future will hold many more vicious attacks on innocent Americans.

There will be prices—in blood, treasure, and peace of mind—to be paid in this contest of wills. But there will be much greater prices to be paid if we do not.

The hardest thing about the coming years will be sustaining our will—and breaking theirs.

Part II

DIMENSIONS OF DEMOCRACY

Two for One

$\mathcal{O}$f the many fascinating aspects about the American political system one is the obsession many commentators have with voter turnout. Every election year editorial writers and pundits flood their media outlets with a great deal of hand-wringing and concern over "low" voter turnout in Maine and the United States.

Why this is so is one of the great mysteries of our age.

Maine usually has one of the highest turnouts of eligible voters in the country (usually around 50 percent in general elections), whatever the election type and whenever they are held. But even here in Maine, no election cycle goes by without great and fervent expressions of concern and predictions that the Republic is heading for decline if not disaster.

Yet nothing could be further from the truth.

First, when I think of high turnouts of voters, I think of the 95 percent plus turnouts that are routinely chalked up in communist countries and dictatorships with some countries in Africa claiming 99.9 percent voter turnout. Nobody should pay any attention to these surrealistic figures. Nobody would think it a good thing if our government forced everybody to vote and then counted the votes of those who didn't any way it wanted.

Second, even when we have had legitimate multiparty democracies with very high turnouts—such as Weimar, Germany—the extremely high turnouts (over 90 percent) often are due to the dangers and fragility of the political system, not a sign of its health. People are petrified that if their side doesn't win, they will lose and lose everything. It is fear, not love of participation, which drives the turnout skyward without artificial inducement.

Now, it is true that the other industrialized democracies in the world have higher voter turnouts than we, but that is usually due to a number of special features of their political system.

First, many only count eligible voters on an election by election basis, not including people in prison in their theoretical totals. In the United States, however, we count all potential voters, including those in prison. Given the U.S. prison population of over three million, we are already in an impossible comparative position when we start counting. We also count legal and illegal aliens, past felons, and people in hospitals in old-age homes as "eligible" voters.

Second, some other countries such as France have voting on Sundays, when few have to work. Were we to switch from Tuesdays to Sundays we would have a much higher percentage of eligible voters. Who wants to do that?

Third, other countries such as Austria and Australia fine non-voters. Were we to start fining those who do not vote $100 or $200, we could increase the vote totals rather easily and impressively. Somehow I doubt Americans would find this a preferable approach to the current individual choice.

But in any case, who cares?

Why should it matter how many people vote in elections?

As long as individuals or groups are not arbitrarily prevented from voting by discriminatory voting requirements, why should anybody care who votes and who doesn't?

More importantly, if someone gives you two votes instead of one, why should you complain? In Maine, even in relatively high turnout elections such as those for president, about 50 percent of eligible voters take the time to exercise their constitutional right.

That means that in most elections in Maine, your vote actually counts twice as much since with half the population not voting, if you take the time and energy to vote, your single vote has twice the impact it would have if everybody voted.

Isn't this a good thing?

Or think about it this way: if every person who is eligible to vote does so, each vote counts 1 percent of the total. But if only 50 percent of the electorate bothers to vote, each vote actually cast counts 2 percent of the hypothetical total.

This means that if you take the time to vote in the next election and only half the eligible voters join you, your vote will be worth twice as much.

Sounds like a pretty good deal to me.

Please don't think I came to this position easily, early, and lightly. More than most, in fact far more than most, going back to 1968 and the Gene McCarthy for President campaign, I have beaten the bushes for voters and tried desperately to get those not registered to vote to do so.

I have gotten more than my fair share of slivers putting up lawn signs (mostly on the lawns of those who wanted to be left alone) and spent more than my fair share of hours on the phones urging greater turnout ("But you can have dinner when you get back from voting").

I think I have more than paid my dues trying to up participation only to find that many Americans take their political system for granted and assume that things will pretty much go along the way they are no matter who wins.

I've come to the conclusion that this is usually a good, not a bad thing because to really get higher turnout in elections, you have to frighten voters with imaginary or not-so-imaginary horribles to get them out of their lethargy and/or their satisfaction and to the polls.

In truth, a democratic political system brings with it responsibilities as well as rights. Voting is one of those. We have the right to vote; we should take the responsibility to vote. But if some of our fellow citizens choose not to exercise their responsibility, why should we care, especially since it gives our own votes more power and cogency?

I also find it fascinating that most commentators assume that those who don't vote, the non-voters, would somehow vote differently.

This is not so in Maine.

In virtually every regular general election I have been able to track in Maine since 1972, the candidate and issue profiles of the non-voter turned out to be quite close to the profile of the actual voter. Obviously this is not necessarily true for special elections or party primaries although even here, the difference between those voters and all voters are usually greatly exaggerated by pundits, commentators, and editors.

So this year, when all the commentators and editorial writers are wringing their hands in anguish and decrying the fate of the Republic, go forth and cast your two votes and count your blessings instead of sheep.

Maine and the Republic will be in good hands.

Free to Be Me

$\mathcal{W}$hy are you a Republican or an Independent or a Democrat? For most voters, the answer in their minds is that when they became old enough, they *chose* to be a member of a particular party, and that this was a rational choice based on issues, style, and a sense of wanting to belong to a group of like-minded people. In fact, I'll bet most readers believe they belong to one party or another based on issues and ideology and a common sense of purpose.

In fact, the literature of political science comes to quite a different conclusion. Starting with the classic 1960 study, *The American Voter* by Angus Campbell, Philip Converse, and others, the literature has been consistent in saying that the single most important influence on party membership is parental partisanship.[1]

In other words, if your parents were Democrats, chances are most likely—at least for the law of large numbers—that you will be a Democrat as well. If your parents were Republican, chances are most likely you are a Republican. Various studies since that time have supported this basic thesis even though there are some obvious current exceptions for the Green and Reform parties.

In my case, the literature seems right on target. My childhood does explain my party affiliation. My father was a building contractor in Hartford, Connecticut. As a small businessman, he was concerned about both big government and big labor. In the post-war period in the Hartford area, organized labor was flexing its muscles and making common cause with the Democratic political establishment

45

in Connecticut. He associated machine politics, corruption, and a lack of concern "for the little guy" with the Democrats.

We also happened to live across the street from Frank Kennelly and his wife Eleanor (and their son Jim) who were all big Democratic activists. Often on Sundays, big black Cadillacs would pull up with Democratic leaders and union heads to plan strategy and set public agendas. John Bailey, for many years the head of the Connecticut Democratic Party and later, when John Kennedy was President, national head of the Democratic Party, would show up as well, sometimes with his daughter Barbara. These Democratic-organized labor get-togethers often spoiled our weekends.

My father would always point these people out to my sister and me and indicate how they were our enemies. They were out to take work away from him, and the Democratic machine was the party that was in alliance with Big Labor. We were Republicans in a sea of Democrats, Scandinavian Lutherans surrounded by Irish Catholics, and small business people at war with big government and especially big labor. In Connecticut in the 1940s, they were synonymous. Democrats controlled most of the major political offices and the legislature and set the local public policy agenda.

I never really understood all this but I certainly accepted my father's point of view, especially after the day in 1950 when he came home and announced that we had to leave the city. We had to move! We had to leave Hartford because the unions and their Democratic bosses were driving him out of business. I was devastated to be leaving my neighborhood and friends. Of course at ten years old, I didn't realize how much more pleasant life would be growing up on the Connecticut shore but powerless and enraged as I was, in true Viking fashion, I promised revenge for my father.

My dad stayed a staunch but moderate Republican all of his life. He became a very tough act to follow in terms of party loyalty. The last year of his life, for example, even suffering from lung cancer and Alzheimer's, he remained a loyal Republican. On Election Day in 1988, I got a frantic call from his nurse who said he'd disappeared. He was lost for several hours before he finally returned home. He'd actually gone to his polling booth in Niantic and stood in line in the rain for a half hour waiting to vote for George Bush. Now that's true party loyalty!

At various times in my life, I've wondered about being something other than a Republican but although I flirted with being a Democrat a couple of times, I've always pulled back at the last moment.

Once was in 1968 when I was teaching at Dartmouth College and Gene McCarthy and then Bobby Kennedy were running for president, but I somehow, even in that year of anti-war activism, ended up in the Republican presidential primary voting for Nelson Rockefeller.

A second time was when I moved back to Maine to teach at Bowdoin College in 1970 and, bitten by the political bug, actually thought I would run for governor as a Democrat. But Bill Cohen talked me out of that truly outrageous idea and asked me to be his campaign manager when he first ran for Congress in 1972, so I stayed a Republican. Also, being outnumbered by 50–1 on the Bowdoin faculty probably also helped to cement my partisan status.

1972 turned out to be very much of a swing year in Maine politics. Maine, for most of the post–World War II period, was a mirror image of Connecticut. In Maine, it was the Republicans who were dominant. In fact, from 1946 until 1960, the Republicans won over 80 percent of the contests for governor, Congress, and the U.S. Senate.

But following the Muskie Revolution of 1954, the Democrats made major inroads into that domination. From 1954 until 1970, they won over half the contests as the personality, drive, and party building of Muskie attracted not only many new Democratic voters but also many new, high quality candidates as well.

After the Cohen counterrevolution of 1972, however, Republicans moved back into the dominant position, winning over 60 percent of the major contests against Democrats, Independents, and Greens. In fact, between 1946 and 1998, Republicans won 64 percent of those contests. Ironically enough, Cohen was not—strictly speaking—a party builder the way Muskie was, but his style, approach, and moderate political philosophy became the model for a whole generation of successful Republican candidates such as Dave Emery, Jock McKernan, Olympia Snowe, and Susan Collins. This entire cohort was very successful with a combined record of eighteen wins and only three losses in general elections.

More recently, political scientists such as Richard Niemi and M. Kent Jennings in their "Issues and Inheritance in the Formation of Party Identification" retested the original parental partisan thesis and found pretty much the same initial results. But they also found that as partisan voters reach middle age, they are more likely to be reenergized and driven by issues and can become free from the weight of parental partisanship.

When I read their findings, I thought they rang true for me as well, but I also had some other impetus for feeling fulfilled.

During the 1998 election cycle, my son Erik, who is with the Republican media firm, Stevens, Reed, Curcio, and Company, worked on the reelection campaign of Republican Connecticut Governor John Rowland.

Rowland's opponent turned out to be Barbara Bailey Kennelly, the Congresswoman from Connecticut Second District where I had grown up. I was dumfounded. Barbara Bailey Kennelly was the Democratic Congresswoman for many years and she had married Jim Kennelly who had lived across the street. Talk about a political dynasty! In Connecticut, "Bailey and Kennelly" was "power plus" and it was her and her team against Rowland and his.

Initially the race was very tight but Rowland's superior television and campaign strategy won the day and Kennelly was crushed 63 percent to 37 percent. On election night, I knew my father (by now in Lutheran heaven) was very pleased and I felt a tremendous sense of closure. Harold Potholm's revenge, after a fashion, had been achieved, not by his son but by his grandson. I felt strangely liberated and light hearted and less partisan than before.

So now, the political science literature and personal closure says I'm free to not be a Republican anymore.

I'm free to become a Democrat, or a Green, or a Reformer (a real option for many Mainers if the Reform Party drafts Angus King to lead the ticket next election cycle).

I'm finally free to pick another party other than the one my parents belonged to.

If I really want to.

NOTE

1. Angus Campbell, Philip Converse , and others, *The American Voter* (New York: Wiley, 1960).

A Clear and Present Danger

The elections of 1999 highlighted two very important dimensions for the future of politics in Maine, dimensions that continue to haunt our political system in the new millennium.

First, Question One, the Partial Birth or Late Term Abortion Ban referendum turned out to be everything voters could ask for. It had dedicated partisans on both sides, activists who worked long and hard to put their side over the top. It had two well-funded campaigns and it had good campaign direction.

The No campaign leaders, Joanne D'Arcangelo and Jeanette Fruen, ran a very strong campaign, one so effective that The Maine Civil Liberties Union is to award Joanne the Roger Baldwin Award this month for "playing a key role in the campaign against the most threatening attempt to limit abortion rights that Maine has experienced."

For their part, Mark Mutty and Teresa McCann Tumidajski of the Yes side did a very good job of keeping their more extreme supporters in line and under cover for most of the campaign and thus had their side in the hunt until the last weekend.

The Yes side enjoyed an early lead—as long as they were able to get voters to concentrate on the procedure itself. But in the last days of the campaign, the No side was able for the first time to get voters to focus on their two basic themes: that the issue was not partial birth abortion but abortion rights, generally, and that this was to be a referendum on the Christian Civic League and the Christian Right's overall social agenda. This combination message resonated powerfully with moderate voters and with those for whom abortion was not a core value, especially men. The late breaking front-page story in the *Bangor Daily News* by Jay Higgins put Mike Heath and the Christian Civic League squarely at the center of the referendum.

By the final weekend of the campaign, it was clear that the higher the turnout the better the No side's chances. While most observers had anticipated a big get-out-the-vote effort from the Catholic Church and the Christian Right, in the end, it was the No side that mounted the most extensive and ultimately most successful get-out-the-vote effort.

With the score 47 percent to 41 percent and little time remaining, the No side mustered an extra $80,000 to mount a huge get-out-the-vote effort (based in Virginia) to energize women who normally do not vote as well as those who always vote. The No side also used TV effectively to gain the swing voters of this election: males.

Whereas women who work at home voted narrowly against the ban (52 percent) and women outside the home voted somewhat more strongly (54 percent) against the ban, it was the male cohort that provided the significant margin of victory. Male voters ended up opposing the ban by a margin of 58 percent, thus sealing its fate.

So the people of Maine were well served. A very contentious issue was well presented by both sides as the partisans did what partisans are supposed to do. When voters get a lively debate with strong supporters on both sides and well-funded campaigns to bring the issues to them, they respond by turning out in higher than expected numbers. Forty-four percent is a very fine turnout for an off-year election and we have both sides on Question One to thank for it.

But in the midst of this good news for democratic participation, there is a second, very ominous development, one which is a threat to the very democratic process we celebrate. That is the rise of censorship by some very shortsighted television station personnel.

Modern elections depend on the thirty-second television commercial. They are the "news" source to which most people pay the most attention. Even newspaper editorials normally have impact in direct relationship to their being put in TV commercials.

That is why it is so pernicious when some individuals take it upon themselves to deny competing points of view their say in the electronic marketplace.

Some Maine stations did very well. Channel 13 and Fox 51 both upheld freedom of speech despite the normal and expected pressures from opposing sides in the abortion debate. Both showed what good station management is all about. They did not try to alter either side's commercials. They stood their ground as both sides brought pressure on them to get into the business of electronic political censorship.

General managers Alan Cartwright and Doug Finck stood tall in the face of political pressure and those who would curtail free speech. They said simply and firmly that free and open debate is vital to our political freedoms.

Channel 13 WGME and Channel 51 WPXI deserve our praise and our viewership.

Unfortunately, that cannot be said for several other TV stations. Several behaved very badly as censorship reared its ugly head in a way I have not seen in thirty years of following Maine elections. Three stations behaved capriciously, some banning one commercial but permitting others, while other stations accepted the banned commercials but then banned others. Basically, three people—none of who are accountable to the public—acted on their own to decide what voters could and could not see.

Steve Thaxton, general manager of Channel 6 (WCSH) and Judy Horan, station manager of Channel 2 (WLBZ) started the parade of folly. Accepting one commercial, but rejecting another which said virtually the same thing, Thaxton hilariously interjected his 7-year-old daughter as arbiter of what was permissible and what was not! He told the Associated Press (AP) that since she saw the commercial on another station and started asking questions about it, that commercial was "out of bounds."

But as inappropriate as the actions of Thaxton and Horan were, they were eclipsed by those of Dave Kaufman, executive vice president of Channel 8 (WMTV). Dave Kaufman took censorship for a strange, often humorous ride. He had previously accepted the commercial banned by Channels 6 and 2. Now he banned the one they then accepted!

In this commercial, "Kellie," a twenty-six-year-old pro-Choice South Portland woman gave her opinion on the proposed partial birth abortion law. Dave decided that Kellie's opinion was not correct and refused to air her commercial.

I believe that with a broadcasting license comes a responsibility, a responsibility to air even unpopular opinions, *especially* unpopular opinions with which one disagrees. One should give opponents the *widest latitude* in stating their case. During the fall, 1999 campaign, I believe Dave Kaufman failed in this responsibility. His initial arbitrary action was not the end of the story however. Far from it. Apparently receiving calls from irate viewers after the AP carried the censorship story, Dave arranged a most bizarre spectacle.

On his own evening news program, Dave had the audacity to have one of his own reporters, Christine Young, interview him—her boss—and toss him incredibly softball questions. It is safe to say that Christine did not live up to her previous reputation for tough, aggressive reporting. While the "interview" was going on, up on the screen was the image of "Kellie," effectively and electronically gagged! If it were not for its serious implications, the incident would have been simply hilarious.

Here he was, the station manager, being interviewed by his own employee while the young woman whose views he has censored was not even present.

Of course TV stations themselves have freedom of speech but that freedom should take the form of editorials, properly identified as such. We would applaud David staking out his position on controversial issues but only properly labeled as editorial comment. It is most inappropriate for station managers to make news and then interpret that news.

Within hours of this command performance, Kaufman next insisted that the No side make a change in one of their commercials. Imagine believing the strange notion that two censored commercials are better than one—or none!

And where was the Maine Civil Liberties Union through all this? You know, the people who defend (correctly) the right of Nazis and KKK members to speak? Strictly AWOL, never raising a hand in the defense of a lone twenty-six-year-old pro-Choice woman who had the audacity to oppose partial birth abortion.

Of course, the MCLU was on the other side of the referendum so the electronic gagging of "Kellie" apparently had to take a back seat to the expediency of the moment. This was not the Maine Civil Liberties Union's finest hour, for when freedom of speech—even electronic speech—is curtailed, we all lose. They, of all people, should know better.

To have supposed ombudsmen like the MCLU abrogate their responsibility just because they are on the other side of a particular issue is very shortsighted and pernicious. It also greatly diminishes their credibility (as well as costing them my donation for this year!). They have every right to vigorously push their own opinions on controversial matters but they *exist* to defend the right of all to do the same.

Significant issues thus remain. Twenty-first century democracy requires the open expression of ideas and paid TV commercials, rightly or wrongly, have become the coin of the political realm. To have station managers deciding what should be aired and what should not in a controversial referendum situation, to set themselves up as judge and jury with no court of appeals, is both capricious and anti-democratic. It also raises suspicions as to whether or not their personal political preferences enter into their decisions. In this context—and irrespective of their rationalizations—who can say why they really act?

Now that the election is over, I hope the people of Maine do not forget and the next time the stations' FCC licenses are set for renewal, we are all there to register our complaints. The corporate owners of Channel 8, the Harron family, and the owners of Channels 6 and 2, The Gannett Corporation, need to know that censorship diminishes the political process and rights of all of us.

Unchecked, censorship of political speech by TV stations represents a clear and present danger to the practice of democracy in the new century. Indeed, in that first election cycle of 2000, Channel 6 in Portland continued to engage in ongoing censorship of ballot measure commercials, intervening several times in the hotly contested Physician-Assisted Suicide public debate.

When a Champion Leaves the Field

There is always sadness when a champion leaves the field.

In recent months, two long term and important players on the Maine political scene have headed for retirement. The departures of both leave the arena less vibrant, less exciting.

John Day, veteran political reporter for the *Bangor Daily News*, recently retired. More than just a reporter, John was a major actor on the Maine political scene for almost forty years.

Beginning in 1963, he toiled on the political beat year after year, both as a reporter and later, a columnist.

More than most political reporters, Day had an excellent sense for a breaking story—and indeed how to present one in most vivid terms. As a result, the *Bangor Daily News* had its share of kudos when he was right and sometimes lawsuits when he was wrong.

Often characterized as a "conservative," Day was regularly harsh on all sectors of the political spectrum and once he got the hint of a story, he seldom let go until it appeared in print. Friendly to a variety of Republicans, Independents, and Democrats, he never hesitated to skewer in print his friends as well as his enemies. Being on his Rolodex was no guarantee of favorable treatment if John felt he had you in his sights.

He was also relentless in his pursuit of his stories. I vividly remember the period in late 1975 when there was intense national and statewide speculation that Bill Cohen, then a Congressman from the Second District, would challenge Senator Ed Muskie in 1976. He knew I was one of the very few close to Bill advising against such a run and he wanted my confirmation that Cohen would not run so he could break the story. For weeks before Cohen's announcement of his decision, John called early and often.

I, of course, could have cared less whether he was right or wrong in his predictions but I was bound and determined not to be "the source." At the same time, I didn't want to lie outright to him, knowing he would never forgive or forget such a transgression so I dodged as many of his calls as I could. The weekend before Cohen's announcement, my wife Sandy and I were skiing with the Cohens at Sugarloaf and John was hot on the trail of the story, following us onto the mountain and skiing wildly to try to catch up with us. He's a better skier now I take it, but that afternoon, he couldn't accomplish his purpose.

I can still see John standing by one of the chairlifts looking this way and that, forcing us to duck onto another trail at the last minute to avoid him. Later, at the end of the day, I even sent an attractive young woman over to ask for his autograph and thus divert him as he stood in front of the lodge while I slipped by in the gathering dusk.

But success eluded me. Somehow he found out where the Cohens were staying and called just as Diane Cohen was making dinner. She answered and chatted with him for a long time, not allowing him to talk to Bill and deftly paring his questions. I remember standing there and wondering why the stuff in the frying pan wasn't burning. By the time she handed the phone to me, Day was in high dungeon. "Damn it, Gordon Manuel (then the anchor on WABI in Bangor) has been on the six o'clock news saying Cohen will run against Muskie. I won't have him scooping me. Is Cohen running or not?"

I looked desperately at Diane, Bill, and my wife. No help there. They were all shaking their heads and smiling, glad I was on the hook, not them. "Well," I said, trying to be noncommittal, "sometimes Manuel is right and sometimes Manuel is wrong." "You son of a bitch, he's not running, is he?" "I can't really say John," I answered, "I have to go now."

I was convinced I had pulled it off. I was convinced he hadn't gotten anything out of me. But the next morning, when Bill began to call his closest supporters prior to his morning news conference to announce his decision, we got quite a shock. Lew Vafiades received the news from Bill with some equanimity. "I know, Bill, " he said, "it's on the front page of the *Bangor Daily News*." Despite our best efforts, Day had broken the story and gotten it right.

John's color and drive and relentlessness will be missed.

Later this spring, Jack Havey of Ad Media will retire as well. Jack's career is as long as Day's and, in many ways, as important to understanding how Maine politics really works. An artist of national renown, Jack has been a major artistic and political player on the Maine scene for over thirty years. Always able to create very vivid, powerful commercials, Jack has had a cogent impact on many political outcomes in the state.

He certainly deserves much of the credit for the 1974 success of Jim Longley Sr., Maine's first Independent governor, coming up with the slogan "Think About It," which resonated so powerfully in the era following Watergate. And his commercial tagline: "You never waste your vote when you vote for the best man," which appeared only the last weekend of the campaign clearly put Longley over the top against his two better-known opponents, Jim Erwin and George Mitchell. I do not believe that Jim Longley would have won that race for governor without Jack Havey in his corner.

Nearly twenty years later, Jack was still creating masterful political commercials when they really mattered. His extremely powerful TV commercials brought state Senator Chuck Cianchette back from the brink of defeat in 1992 after he was targeted by the AFL/CIO in the Democratic primary. On one Saturday morning in a Portland edit suite, Jack captured the essence of Chuck and created a very moving set of commercials which went to the very heart of why Chuck was an extraordinary man with wonderful vision for the future of Maine.

Jack and his firm (including Beryl-Ann Johnson, Kathy Guerin, Judy Small, and for many years, John Christie) were highly successful in the ballot measure arena as well. His strong and effective ads, for example, made the difference in the Elected Public Utilities struggle of 1981 and the Save Maine Yankee II contest of 1982.

And I firmly believe that he single-handedly developed the strategy and created the imagery that defeated the Equal Rights Amendment in 1984. He took a relatively unknown Bowdoin professor, Richard Morgan, and put him in front of a brick building in Massachusetts ("If they think it's Bowdoin College, who am I to argue with them?").

Morgan, calmly and rationally, but with considerable authority and gravitas, asked voters to think about all the implications of the proposed law. Support for the ERA, which had been running at 3–1, diminished with each passing day of Jack's TV and the ad was so effective that the Bowdoin faculty was asked by supporters of the ERA to consider a college bylaw prohibiting professorial involvement in TV commercials! Fortunately, calmer heads prevailed and Bowdoin professors kept their First Amendment rights.

But in the middle of this smashing success, Jack showed considerable political courage. When national opponents of the ERA came to Maine and engaged in what he took to be vicious, anti-gay attacks, Jack called a statewide press conference to denounce both the tactics and those supporters. "I don't want to win if that is what it takes to succeed," he said.

In the end, he won the ERA battle but as in so many other situations, Jack remained true to himself and his values. I learned a great deal from Jack and the Ad Media team. In fact, with the possible exceptions of Chuck Winner and Henry Kissinger, I learned more about political consulting from Jack Havey than anyone else.

Jack's strengths were not just his artistic ability or his personal courage. They also included a core value that I have never forgotten. Jack always kept control over the campaign and believed most strongly that it was better to lose making your own mistakes than to let your client do something that was against your better judgment. I often called him "The Sun King" for the warmth of his personality, the size and lavishness of his retinue, and his ability to burn clients to a crisp if they did things he thought were against their—or his—best interests.

Jack passed up a lot of corporate and political clients—and let others already in his stable go elsewhere—sticking to his credo. But he was always true to himself and his sense of what should be done. He always wanted the client to be successful, not simply comfortable. He always wanted the best effort put into every TV commercial. He wanted the best commercials, not just the ones the client liked.

I never hear the Frank Sinatra song "I Did It My Way" without thinking of Jack Havey. Since 1962, he did it his way and taught the rest of us the meaning of integrity in consulting and how to manage clients without compromising your core values. In the political history of Maine, Jack Havey will always be a player.

He will be missed on many fronts.

It is always sad when a champion leaves the field, but the real blessing and consolation is that you had the opportunity to watch that champion perform and learned from his or her achievements.

Gratitude

*W*ebster's Dictionary defines "gratitude" as "a feeling of thankful appreciation for favors or benefits received; thankfulness."

On this score and on this date, my cup runneth over.

First, I am very grateful for all the readers who took the time to call, e-mail, and write me about my cousin Charles Petersen and my column about his gallant fight against cancer. It is very clear that he touched many lives with his courage and humor, his faithfulness to his job, and his love for his family, friends, and students. Somehow, hearing from others about what Charlie meant to them helps to ease the burden of his passing.

I especially appreciated all the friends of Charlie's sharing with me the fond memories of his spirit and his life. Just about everyone commented on his positive attitude toward life and many said they were unaware of the extent of his physical condition. "He never complained" one fellow teacher said. Noteworthy among the many acts of kindness was that of Secretary of Defense William S. Cohen. Bill took time out of his very busy schedule to not only send a personal note to Charlie's wife Marlene, but also to get President Clinton to send her a fine written tribute commemorating Charlie's service to his country. Both mean a great deal to her as she copes with her loss.

Second, I was very grateful for Bill's invitation to my wife and I to attend the 4th of July festivities on the USS Kennedy in New York harbor. Flying up from Andrews Air Force base to New York City on his command plane was a terrific thrill (and one I know Charlie was with me in spirit). It was the first plane ride I've ever been on that I did not want to end. Bill and his wife Janet Langhart were gracious hosts and the subsequent motorcade through New York City with red lights flashing and NYPD's finest riding herd was very enjoyable. The whole trip was a magic carpet ride from beginning to end.

Bill has long repaid Sandy and I for whatever help we were able to provide in his elections to Congress and the Senate and I'm sure there were many from Washington's social A list who would have killed for an invitation to this trip. What made it so special was that Bill reached out and extended himself to make us feel so welcome and at the center of the entire affair.

We also appreciated the many kindnesses of Bill's chief of staff, Bob Tyrer. For those readers who know Bob as campaign manager for Susan Collins as well as for his twenty-five years of service to Bill Cohen, it was a delight to watch him coordinate his staff, the various security details, and interface with the president's entourage, and still find time to share stories from his Maine campaigns. Watching him deep in consultation with His Royal Highness Prince Bandar Bin Sultan of Saudi Arabia, using the same skills he'd honed practicing on the Maine Republican State Committee and John Day was itself worth the trip.

The 4th of July was a long day, beginning at 5:00 AM and ending at midnight, and included a ferry ride out to the USS Kennedy where 8,000 people watched the parade of the tall ships, the fly-over of many aircraft, and the arrival of the president who subsequently took the salutes from the many vessels, foreign and American. Attorney General Janet Reno swore the oath of citizenship for a dozen of our newest citizens and there were numerous performances by Broadway casts. *People* magazine would have had a field day with the assorted celebrities wandering around on the flight deck. They ranged from Caroline Kennedy Schlosberg and Dr. Ruth, to Miss America and Sandy Potholm, Senators John Glenn, Gary Hart, and Ed Brooke, as well as Sam Donaldson and Deepak Chopra.

President Clinton gave a warm welcoming speech and paid tribute to the armed forces. Through it all, Bob Tyrer made sure we had terrific seats and the company of a three star admiral, Greg "Grog" Johnson, the secretary of defense's senior military assistant. The admiral may also have been selected simply to make sure we didn't get lost in the crowd or wander too close to the edge of the flight deck and fall off. I have never served in the military but I quickly noticed that with a three-star admiral leading the way, the crowds parted like the Red Sea. And had we been on our own, I doubt the captain of the ship would have let us relax in his air conditioned cabin when it got too hot on deck.

After the president finally helicoptered off the ship, the sailors went back to work and most of the visitors had left, the secretary's party had a dinner on the flight deck. It was a truly magic moment. To be dining in the open air, with a band and terrific food and even better company, and see the Statue of Liberty glowing at sunset was a moment to treasure for a lifetime.

Bill and Janet both gave stirring speeches thanking the crew and all the armed forces for their efforts. All day long, the crew and their families couldn't wait to meet Bill and his wife and to shake their hands. The Navy's close order drill team put on a very impressive demonstration that ended just about the time the fireworks began. As for the fireworks, I have never seen such a display. In fact, I read later that it was the biggest fireworks display ever! It certainly looked like it.

All in all, it was the most glorious Fourth I've ever had! Or as Dick Carlson, the former U.S. ambassador to the Seychelles, put it in the next day's *Washington Post*, "It sure beats barbecuing in the back yard and running around with sparklers."

But beyond the joys of the day and the delights of the trip itself, I found myself feeling very grateful for what the day really represented. We always read about problems in the military. We hear about cost overruns and difficulties of this or that weapon's system. But we seldom stop to see what the American military presence really is all about. Or what position and lifestyle we in America would enjoy without that presence.

I wish everyone could have stood on that deck and reflected on what our liberty means and how big a contribution our armed forces make toward preserving it. To see a small part of our armed forces doing such a magnificent job reinforced my respect for and pride in all of them.

This was one aircraft carrier with a crew of five thousand. We have twelve, protecting American interests in the Atlantic, Pacific, Indian oceans, the Mediterranean Sea, and the Arabian Gulf. Some are always on station, others are being refitted, and others are in port to give their crews a rest. It is difficult to comprehend the logistics that must be mounted to keep the various fleets in operation 365 days a year.

This Fourth focused on the Navy and to a lesser extent the Air Force, but think of the hundreds of thousands—even millions—of American men and women in the Army, Navy, Air Force, Marines, and Coast Guard who are scattered all around the globe, protecting American interests and keeping the global peace.

We may not have set out to lead the world's hegemony but it is difficult to say any other country would or could have played the role any better.

I was born during World War II, grew up during the Korean War, became an adult during the Vietnam War, and celebrated our success in the Gulf War. We can argue about this or that dimension of this or that war but the bottom line is so many Americans have died to protect all of us from harm and from foreign domination and to preserve the many freedoms we often take for granted.

Many took—and still take—big chunks out of their lives to serve and protect. Seeing the young men and women on the USS Kennedy— eager, efficient, and effective—made me appreciate how many pieces of how many lives are always on the line to protect our country and its interests. I am, by nature, more than a little cynical but seeing the crew of the USS Kennedy and their families, sharing their pride and a few moments of their service time, it was impossible not to feel uplifted and appreciative of the security the American military provides.

I was also struck by the spirit and motivation of the crew. Dozens of them expressed the same thought when complimented on the quality of the ship or their performance. "It's your ship," they would say, or "This ship belongs to the people, all of the people." The Cohen legacy no doubt.

Think about that for a moment: how many navies in the world today—let alone in history—have such an ethos?

When we get caught up in the wrangles about budgets and weapon systems and procurement problems, it is far too easy to overlook the benefits, direct and indirect, we all derive from the American military. They are there for us, in peace as in war, and their being there in peace makes it less likely there will be a war.

Standing on that carrier deck at dusk on the 4th of July, it was impossible not to feel gratitude to all those who served and all those who still serve and who will serve to preserve and protect our country and our way of life.

We are well served.

My McKinley

In 1896, a man named William McKinley of Ohio ran for president. He was elected. He campaigned hardly at all and most of that was done from his front porch. He is my model for this chapter in the saga of Maine politics. More important still, he is the model for my wife Sandra who wants to do good things for people she likes under the so-called "Clean Elections" Act. But she doesn't want to leave her porch to do so.

2002 will be the first gubernatorial race held under the dictates—and possibilities—of the so-called Clean Elections Act. Of course the title is but a crude effort to position the law as something good for the citizens of the state. On the contrary; it will, I believe, be remembered as something very good for political consultants.

In fact, in order to be more accurately titled, the so-called Clean Elections Act should be renamed the "Bay Buchanan Full Employment Act for Consultants" in honor of the sister and campaign manager of Pat Buchanan who ran on $12 million dollars of federal funds (i.e. our tax dollars) and had a wonderful time. She is my mentor.

Under Maine's new election law, anyone—and I mean anyone—can run for governor and get tax dollars to pay for their campaign. In fact, assuming any candidate doesn't opt for the tax dollars and raises a reasonable amount of money on their own, *all* "clean" candidates get up to $1.2 million dollars! Talk about a socialistic approach to politics that smart capitalists can take advantage of. Talk about a dream for political consultants.

Now to date, most of the articles and commentary about the law have focused on the "cause" candidates such as Jonathan Carter and Mike Heath who, for the first time, will have millions of dollars to push their—thus far—narrow agendas. Jonathan Carter, for example, will undoubtedly run for governor both to win (he could be elected with only 28 percent of the vote) and to push his radical environmental agenda.

Mike Heath and anyone else who feels like it can also run to push their own or their group's agenda or cause. In the past, fringe candidates and fringe causes have been limited by their inability to raise funds (a measure of support) and thus the political system has had a centrist character.

How about George Smith? Why not have a candidate for sportsmen and women? Why not have someone spending $1.2 million of taxpayer money to promote the interests of those who hunt and fish?

So the new law will promote lots of new "cause" candidates and further reduce the power of the Republican and Democratic parties. This is good or bad, depending on your view of how things are in the state and whether a movement toward socialized elections makes sense or not.

But my initial insight into the Act is at once more exciting and more engaging, to say nothing of potentially lucrative. It focuses on the ease with which political consultants can now find candidates, run them for governor, and get very well paid for their effort. They can even run themselves if they cannot get other people to do so.

You see, under the new law, it is very easy to raid the public treasury. Very easy indeed. You only need to get 2,250 people to give $5 to your candidate. That may sound like a lot if you personally have to go door to door to get it but if you hire a fundraiser—on speculation even—you can get that amount very quickly. Who wouldn't put up $10,000 in order to get up to $1.2 million?

So forget third party candidates and other cause people. The pot of gold under the political rainbow is now available to any consultant smart enough to take advantage of the new law.

I'm quite sure that if I've thought of this there are dozens of other consultants out their licking their chops and ready to roll.

Here's how I would, could, and perhaps even will do it.

First, I have a great candidate. My wife Sandra is liked by just about everybody. She enjoys people and would make a good impression. And she's been my campaign manager for life. She's into nutrition and health and nurturing. She's a wonderful person. True, she doesn't like public speaking but that's not important under the new rules. Not important at all. What is key, she has faith in my ability to put bread on the table so she might well like this idea and its payoffs for those she loves and she might become my candidate.

The fact that she would not like to run as a politician and go flying all over the state meeting with voters and running herself ragged isn't an impediment. She won't have to. Under the new law, she, like McKinley, can announce and run and stay on her front porch. In fact, she can, if she wants, stay there until the October 2002 debates when she can go on TV and talk up her interests and causes.

By then, she'll be well known because I can put together a dream team. In fact, it wouldn't have to be a dream team at all, just a team, but I'd like to start with the best to get to that $1.2 million first.

There's George Smith of "Mainely Maine" and Edie Smith. I'll want them to do the petition gathering and as much fundraising as they can. They're very good at what they do and being good Republican entrepreneurs, undoubtedly willing to work for little up-front money in the hopes of a huge and guaranteed payday later on. They've been at it since 1974 and been very successful so they'll be a huge asset to the campaign.

Then there's George Campbell of PA Strategies. He's a great fundraiser as well as being an engaging and terrific person. With his associate Keith Citron, he'll raise a ton of money. In fact, I've spoken to him already and he thinks raising $10,000 via $5 contributions is a snap and he's ready to go. In my experience, George and Keith are the top fundraising team in the state and will deliver on their promises to Sandy and me.

Once Sandy is on the ballot, and we have a steady stream of tax dollars coming our way, steady, reliable, and a lot of them, we can really spring into action.

I've already signed myself up to do the polling. Sandy's run for governor in 2002 will be the best-tracked effort in history. Not just Maine history. History. Period. We will poll for her monthly, weekly, daily, even hourly. Not even Bill Clinton ever had as much high quality polling as we are going to have. She'll know just how much progress she's making every hour on the hour. Dave Emery will test key precincts that don't even know they are key precincts!

Sandy's also selected her media consultant—her son Erik. Erik did the commercials in 2000 for the Forest Referendum and the Assisted Suicide Referendum so he knows how to get the attention of Maine people. He tells me that production costs will be high, however, creating another *Gone with the Wind* to promote his mother's candidacy.

Press relations will be handled by our daughter, Heather. Heather currently works with special needs children so taking care of the press corps should be, if you'll pardon the expression, child's play.

Sandy's parents, John and Claire Quinlan, although in their eighties, will handle the field work. In fact, with my McKinley, they won't have to do much field work at all but we will pay them very well. They can ride around in their car and go all over Maine, stopping for lunch or overnight or gas and chatting up their daughter's candidacy. After all, these are their figurative golden years, and with the so-called Clean Elections Act these can become their literal golden years as well.

And so it goes. We'll spend the $1.2 million easily enough and have a lot of fun doing it. Sandy will get a little name recognition and make a lot of people close to her very happy.

The only problem I see as a political consultant is that the $1.2 million will go very quickly. My task now is to get the Legislature to up the amount of public funds available per candidate to $3 million or $5 million.

This should be easy to do. These government give-a-way programs always start small and then grow and grow and grow. And since the Legislature will have no control over how many candidates can declare themselves "clean" and thus their consultants "rich," if enough consultants move smartly, we can really raid the treasury before anybody wakes up to this.

Even then, there isn't much anybody can do about it, even those people who see this as a farce and fiasco. That's because, and here's the real beauty of this full employment act for consultants, who's going to dare stand up and say the "Clean Elections" Act is not socialism, but rogue capitalism at its best?

This can go on and on and on. No more relying on two or three candidates: we consultants can have one candidate for every consultant, field, polling, media, fundraising, etc. The more the merrier. Politics is no longer a zero-sum game. It's a wide-open free-for-all and consultants will be very, very happy; it's part of the political landscape.

I just want to get there first and set the standard. And it'll be a gold one, I can assure you.

Maine.

Now it's "the way life should be" for consultants as well as others.

My McKinley will make it so.

Part III

ANALYZING DEMOCRACY

Playing King Lear

$\mathscr{P}$olitics is—and should be—a lot of fun.

Although it is about serious matters, the game of politics is played by human beings with many foibles and defects as well as many admirable qualities. Nobody should take politics as seriously as die-hard partisans, the Democrats who can find no good in any Republican, the Republicans who can find no good in any Democrat, or the Green Party member who finds both Republicans and Democrats beyond the pale. No party or group of activists has a monopoly on political truth and none should act as if they do.

Bill Cohen and I were at Bowdoin College at the same time and in the same fraternity. In those days and for a decade or so after we graduated in 1962, Bill was considered to be in "my" class. But now, of course, and much to my chagrin, I am considered to be in "his" class! Anyway, while in college, we spent a lot of time discussing life, politics, the mysteries of the universe, girls, and sex (although perhaps not in that order).

Oddly enough, considering where we both ended up, neither of us took any government courses and neither of us showed the slightest interest in student government. Indeed, both of us found it very hard to believe that the National Lampoon's movie *Animal House* was about Dartmouth, not the Bowdoin we knew. We loved it.

After we graduated in 1962, Bill and I both ended up doing graduate work in the Boston area, he at Boston University law school and I at the Fletcher School of Law and Diplomacy. We continued many of our conversations that we had begun as undergraduates.

71

Two concepts in particular came out of those conversations, concepts that have stayed with me since.

The first is Bill's notion of "the thin membrane." In those days, Bill not only wrote poetry, he read it and somewhere along the way, he latched on to "the thin membrane," a simple but powerful metaphor for the fragility and fleeting nature of life. The thin membrane could be the lining of your stomach or your lungs or your skin and by extension, any small misstep that could take your life. This was a sobering thought, and for a follower of Loki, the Norse god of mischief, a concept in real life which always needs to be balanced by an appreciation of the comic, the absurd, the hilarious.

The second concept was a message Bill picked up from a lecture by E.G. Marshall, the talented stage and TV actor. Asked how he could play the part of a character with whom he did not agree, Marshall replied that "you don't have to believe in regicide to play King Lear." Both Bill and I were fascinated by the concept as well as by the aplomb with which Marshall delivered it and for me at least, "you don't have to believe in regicide to play King Lear" has come to have a great deal of relevance over the years.

Ending up as a college professor and political activist, I have always remembered Marshall's dictum. To me, being a college professor means that while you may have personal preferences and positions, you must not only see both—or all—sides in a political debate, you are honor bound to present those sides when a student comes with her or his point of view. It is your duty in the classroom to challenge your own ideas as well as those which you oppose. In fact, there is a pedagogical imperative which demands you challenge your own ideas most of all and by playing the devil's advocate at all times, you best serve the process of education.

I fear this notion is regarded as quaintly old fashioned by many of my colleagues. Having taught over the years at a variety of places such as Tufts, Vassar, Dartmouth, the College of the Virgin Islands, and the University of Southern Maine, as well as at my alma mater Bowdoin College, I have always been surprised by how many professors have a definite political point of view to which they expect their students to adhere. They take themselves and their political points of view far too seriously and stereotype their "opponents" far too easily and permanently with a reflexive label of "liberal" or "conservative."

I guess when it comes to these matters, I'm more of an old-fashioned liberal, the kind who cherishes political debates for what one can learn from the debate, not just hearing yourself state what you already know. I believe there is no absolute political truth.

I think one needs to challenge all students on their political positions and make them defend them to the best of their ability regardless of whether or not they agree with you and yours. I think it is ethically wrong to make students adhere to a political philosophy just because it happens to be yours or because you think it is "right." I think you are duty bound to see the relevance and appeal of the very ideas and concepts you oppose.

I teach a course in Maine politics at Bowdoin and each fall, every member of that class has to follow a political campaign closely, getting involved and taking responsibility for that campaign in class discussions. These can be either candidate campaigns or one of the host of ballot measures for which Maine is becoming quite famous.

National players now come from far and wide to participate in Maine's ballot measures and with each passing election cycle, more and more national groups, consultants, and workers come into the state to participate either behind the scenes or many times out front.

For example, those people who want to bring physician-assisted suicide to Maine are going to draw a great deal on the help of people from California to try to make their case to the electorate and those who oppose it will undoubtedly draw upon the talents of people from Oregon or Michigan.

There is a lot of political action in Maine every year and those eighteen to twenty-one-year-old students need to get out and participate in real campaigns with real elections, real voters, and real outcomes. Elections have a good and finite quality to them. Somebody wins (at least for this election cycle) and somebody loses (at least momentarily), but the process itself provides a priceless learning experience. Your ideas may not have been wrong, you may simply have failed to get them across to the people who showed up to vote.

But in assigning students to particular campaigns, I insist they follow and work for candidates or causes *with whom or which they do not agree*. If they are Republicans, they have to work for some other party's candidate. If they are Democrats or Greens, the same thing applies. I don't like them to feel comfortable and just do what they would have done before they took the course

If they favor physician-assisted suicide, they must work for the opposition. If they oppose physician-assisted suicide, they must work on the side that wishes to pass it. Greens have to work against Jonathan Carter in whatever "eco-foolishness" he is currently trying to pedal, and budding young conservatives are expected to get some green behind their ears and help the same Jonathan Carter in his current "crusade for justice and right in the forest."

Initially, students don't like this approach one bit. Many of them are used to mouthing slogans and delivering superficial judgments on candidates, parties, philosophies, and just about everything else under the sun. Many offer the most shallow of solutions. They are uncomfortable looking too closely at, let alone working for, a candidate they "don't like" or against a cause they "believe in." But for one semester and in one course, they have to play King Lear no matter whether they approve of monarchy or regicide or not.

Many complain, often to me, sometimes to the Dean of Student Tranquility, a relatively new post in the Mr. Rogers/Sesame Street era of higher education, a position dedicated to the quaint notion that one should never feel uneasy about anything or find learning anything but sheer low key, rewarding fun!

But no matter. If they want to pass the course, they need to stretch a bit. Well, often more than a bit. They may even have to *memorize* some things (like the counties in Maine or the reach of Portland versus Bangor TV). When most of us went to college in the 1950s and 1960s we expected that we would have to memorize some dates and facts and not just rely on how we felt about an issue or a candidate. Very little memorization goes on in secondary education today and it shows in many of the students who go on to higher education.

Interestingly enough, when the semester is over, virtually all the students say they have learned more than they thought they would from this method or role reversal. Most have learned valuable life lessons of intellectual tolerance and respect for one's opponents.

Playing King Lear in a single play doesn't have to make you believe in regicide but it does force you to look at old issues in new ways or new issues in old ways.

Here is a lesson for all partisans, not just young ones. The Maine political system is wide open to talent. Virtually every cause and every candidate in a year's election cycle will welcome participation. There are dedicated men and women who believe and should believe in their causes. But it is a rare individual who cannot learn from putting him or herself in his or her opponent's position and seeing the possible good in their endeavors or even motives. No individual or group or cause has a monopoly on political truth. All have something to contribute to our ongoing political process and system.

We all benefit when we are more tolerant ideologically.

So too does the political system.

Polling 101

$\mathcal{T}$here are few aspects about a political campaign which are as interesting to me as polling. Polls are such a part and parcel of modern political campaigns and the news coverage of them that it is hard for me to think of political activity without them. Sometime ago, a good friend of mine called. He was anxious to run for the state senate against a popular incumbent, one who had been returned to office by margins of over 60 percent. My friend was wondering aloud where he should campaign, what should be his principle message, and even what his lawn signs should say.

We were well into the discussion when I asked him if he planned to do a public opinion poll to determine where he stood in relationship to his opponent and to identify those "wedge" issues, the ones that would separate him from his opponent. The surprised tone in my friend's voice indicated he'd not even considered doing a poll. And later, when he said he would have to talk to his "advisors" to see if they thought it would be a good idea, I knew he was about to thrash around in campaign mode without a cognitive map of the district.

There is a Chinese saying: "If you don't know where you're going, any road will take you there." That really says all one needs to know about the importance of high quality polling in politics. Candidates—and supporters of causes—need a cognitive map of the electorate so they can use their scarce resources: their limited funds, their limited media opportunities, and above all, their limited time—to the best advantage. Polling is necessary to take them toward, not away from, their goal object. Why more candidates and more causes don't use this tool is beyond me.

Yet many enter political contests without such guidance. Some are successful (especially if their opponent is not armed with polling data either), but many are not. Especially when challenging an incumbent, one needs to have all the help one can get. Identifying the issues that separate one from one's opponent is critical. After all, why should the electorate turn their back on someone who is already in office unless you can give them a reason to turn them out of office? So polls really are essential to the running of successful, cost effective campaigns especially against incumbents.

Polls are also now part and parcel of media coverage of contests. Most major daily newspapers in the state of Maine come up with some kind of polling at some point during political campaigns while many television stations do the same. These efforts usually make news, no matter how mundane or erroneous their findings and most put them on the front page or lead the news with their conclusions.

Yet few reporters or editors seem to know more than the basics of polling and hence their coverage of even their own polls often leads to erroneous conclusions. Most reporters take the majority of newspaper and television polls as "true" because they were done by a disinterested third party. The most serious flaw in their handling of these public polls often has to do with a misunderstanding of what it takes to make a valid poll.

What gives polls their accuracy is the randomness of the survey. That is to say, how were the people chosen by the polling entity? The more random the selection, the more accurate the conclusions. On one level, you can use telephone books and select every 100th or 1,000th name. Call that person and then the next 100th or 1,000th and so on until you have completed the survey.

But this method has a major drawback. Over 10 percent of the population now has unlisted telephones so this group—often the voters most likely to turn out to vote—would not even be included in the universe of calls made. A much better approach is to have a computer randomly select telephone numbers from among all possible telephone numbers in the necessary exchanges.

This can be more expensive for the pollster because you can't filter out businesses or other nonproductive telephone numbers just by looking at the number and name as you can with a telephone book, but it does result in superior accuracy.

Once the computer has selected the numbers, however, you have to make sure you do everything you can to stick to those numbers. You need to call back three or four times if there is no answer at a given number because it is the randomness of the selection which provides the accuracy enabling one to make statements about the results you get.

When the polling results are in, there is a mathematical formula, which indicates how accurate they are. The degree of accuracy is qualified by a term known as the "margin of error." You often see this in the newspaper along with the polling results or it is announced by the TV personality. "Margin of error" means that if the survey has 400 respondents in it, it is said to have a possible error of plus or minus 5 percent. Thus if candidate X is said to have 45 percent of the vote, he or she really could have 40 percent or 50 percent.

The margin of error thus shows the range within which the survey results fall. If the survey had five hundred respondents, the margin of error is plus or minus 4 percent and if 250, it is plus or minus 6 percent. And remember, these margins of error are only applicable for two choice questions, a "yes" or a "no," or candidate X versus candidate Y. If there are more candidates or choices than two, the margin of error goes up accordingly.

Also, because most reporters, editors, and TV personalities don't give the range of possibilities, people tend to think that the base number is fixed, that is it is really 45 percent, not the range of 40 percent to 50 percent if 400 people were called. This penchant for accepting the base numbers at face value can lead to a lot of confusion (and consternation among candidates and their supporters) if new polling shows other results.

Let's say that the candidate who had 45 percent in the first poll is said in a second, later poll to have only 40 percent (with the same margin of error), most people (and candidates) would interpret the data as saying candidate X was losing ground. In fact, there may have been no movement at all within the electorate; the candidate really may have had 42 percent all along and the first survey placed him or her too high and the second too low. So much confusion about polling results could be cleared up if the media outlets presented polling data to the public as a range of possible outcomes, not a single outcome.

But there is an even bigger caveat, which should be explained, and one that almost never is announced by anybody, including most pollsters. That is the extent to which the mathematical tables used to compute the margin of error are based on a .95 confidence factor. That means the margin of error is valid BUT only in 95 out of 100 cases. This is actually a very high probability, but it still means that in 5 out of 100 cases, the poll will be totally off! I have yet to see this caveat on any published poll in the state of Maine during the last thirty years. But it does explain some polls that were way, way off the mark during that time.

There is also another aspect of polling head-to-head contests between candidates which is seldom understood by the news media. Over the years I have tried and tried to get reporters to ask the following question. "Ok, so the poll says you have 56 percent and your opponent has 26 percent—that's among all respondents. What are the head-to-head numbers among respondents *who know both candidates?*" Incumbents almost always have big leads over their opponents when the race begins and for most of its duration, but those leads are often inflated by what is called "name recognition factor."

Since "recognition" is easier than "recall," most voters will pick the name they know if they are unsure about the challenger and that in and of itself gives the incumbent or better-known candidate a seeming advantage in many polls.

If reporters would only insist that the campaign pollster or even the station or newspaper's own pollster give both numbers, they and their readers or viewers would have a much better idea of how the horse race was coming. When Angus King ran against Joe Brennan in 1994, when the race began, Brennan had a huge lead, something on the order of 48 percent to 9 percent. Many people assumed that King was better known than he was, having been on public television for so long. In fact, only about 13 percent of the electorate knew who he was.

But among voters who knew both King and Brennan, the horse race was actually in King's favor, giving him the hope that as more and more people knew who he was, the better he would do since Brennan's huge lead was based in part on his high name recognition and King's lack of recognition.

The candidate behind in the polls often has a difficult time getting the press to give any credibility to his or her campaign when the overall polls show him or her way behind. But if the reporters would only go one step farther, they would have a much better idea of the upside potential of the lesser-known candidate who trails the better-known one. And we would have more engaging and probably closer contests.

The press corps, especially the print media, does tend to take polls seriously and their own handicapping of the candidates even more seriously. These reporters talk among themselves and get an idea fixed in their heads who is going to win and who is not and they often treat those they perceived as losing as less credible, hence they give them less coverage and show less interest in whatever they are saying (however desperate they may sound at this juncture in the campaign). They often privately pronounce this or that candidate as "dead" even before the election is held.

The pithiest expression I ever heard about this phenomenon was Harry Richardson who was running for governor in 1974 against the better-known Jim Erwin and the lesser-known Wakine Tanous. Various polls had been in the newspapers showing him losing to Erwin by a large margin, roughly 3–1, when in fact among voters who knew both, the contest was a virtual tie. In the waning stages of the campaign, Richardson had a meeting with Fred Nutter, then news director for Channel 6, WCSH. "How did it go?" we asked Harry after his meeting. "Fred was very nice," said Harry, "he treated me the way you would somebody with terminal cancer; he acted very sorry for my situation." Harry lost the primary but by only 500 votes. His campaign was written off just as it was hitting its stride.

As we proceed toward the important elections of 2002 and more and more polling data becomes available, readers should ask themselves about the process and outcomes of particular polls in order to understand exactly what is happening as opposed to what appears to be happening.

More Polling Observations

In this chapter, we examine some additional concepts that help us to understand the art and the science of polling.

First, it is very true that some candidates run without polling and some are successful without this tool. The 2000 candidacy of John McCain is a case in point. Not only did John McCain do no polling, he made a virtue out of the fact that he didn't. Many people said they liked that about him and found him refreshing. Still, his opponent, George W. Bush, did extensive polling and was ultimately able to position himself—rightly or wrongly—as the candidate of the Republicans who voted rather than the candidate of the Democrats and Independents. Without polling, especially exit polling, there would have been no way to make that claim stick. The networks ended up validating Bush's statement with their own exit polling numbers.

Second, the truly amazing success of the Clinton presidency—at least in public approval terms—underscores what a strong weapon good polling can be. Clinton simply polls and polls and polls so he always knows where a majority of the American people is. He jumps on popular issues and jumps away from unpopular ones much like a big, happy bullfrog in a pond with large, strong lily pads and other small, weak ones. Sometimes he does it so fast and so skillfully, he doesn't even get his feet wet. With all his jumping around, national Republicans often look slow and clueless, stuck with the smaller, less desirable lily pads.

Third, the recent debate in the Maine Legislature over gun control highlights another very important aspect of polling. It is true that a majority of Mainers say they like more "gun control." When gun control is linked to such emotionally laden aspects as spousal abuse or preventing children from having access to guns by putting locks on them, the support levels for gun control go even higher.

But, as supporters of gun control such as Maine Citizens against Handgun Violence found out to their dismay most recently, public opinion is not simply about a popular attitude.

One has to take into account the *intensity* of that attitude. By that I mean the fervor with which an opinion is held. Many people may believe in the abstract notion of "gun control." They may also believe in some specific aspects of gun control. But they usually don't do much about it, while those who oppose both "gun control" and the specific aspects of it, generally hold their values more intensely, make opposition to gun control one of their core values and act accordingly.

Thus, while many people favor gun control, it is very seldom either the top issue for them or even an issue on which they will pick a candidate. Instead, it is the anti-gun control people who have gun control in their minds as one of the central issues in what makes them a voter and they will both reward a candidate who agrees with them and punish one who does not. Legislators know the difference and that is why so many of them claimed to be listening to their constituents when they voted against gun control. They were, in fact, listening to the intensity of those who opposed gun control.

Supporters of gun control almost always fail to appreciate the importance of this intensity when planning their political battles when they simply look at the surface numbers and conclude that because they have the numbers, they should win the argument. Intense opinions on gun control, like those on abortion, have long histories, are well defined for hard-core believers, and are almost impossible to change.

By contrast, the widely varying polls in various newspapers about the issue of physician-assisted suicide speak to another dimension of polling. Some polls have shown Maine people supporting the issue, often by a large margin, while others have Maine people opposing the concept of physician-assisted suicide. It may be the way in which the question was asked on a particular poll or how it was preceded and followed by other questions. Either aspect often pushes people one way or the other.

But it is also because physician-assisted suicide is a relatively new concept for the electorate in Maine. Most voters have not had much of a chance to put the issue in perspective for themselves. Thus, public opinion on this issue can be said to be *fluid*, that is likely to change over time as people become more familiar with the concept. Partisans on both sides seek to *harden*, or make firmer, public opinion favorable to their side of the issue even as they endeavor to convert those who are undecided.

Another important aspect of polling which is relevant to the current political scene is the *distribution* of opinion or how that opinion is distributed through the voting population. For example, both Jane Amero, the Republican, and Mark Lawrence, the Democrat, were much less widely known than the incumbents they challenged. Representative Tom Allen was much better known than Jane Amero and Senator Olympia Snowe was much better known than Mark Lawrence. This is true even though both Amero and Lawrence had held prominent positions in the legislative leadership in Augusta.

For the challengers, the distribution of opinion is currently not in their favor, for it is not as widespread as the support for their opponents, the incumbents. How can they make up the difference? First, they need to get more widely known. Consequently, we can expect to see the challengers calling press conferences and sending out press releases to try to get up their name identification.

Second, if they have done polling—and I assume they both have—they have probably used what is called an *informed ballot* to help them position themselves. They will have given the voters surveyed some adjectives and characteristics to help those who have never heard of them personally indicate whether or not if the attribution became known to them, would they like them more than the incumbent?

Realizing that their opponents are much better known, they have probably asked a series of questions designed to show their upside potential by putting various clues with his or her name. For example, Mark Lawrence will have asked voters who they favor: "Mark Lawrence" or "Olympia Snowe."

But he probably also used their respective offices to see if that made a difference in the relative levels of support. He may have asked voters, for example, whether they favored "Senate President Mark Lawrence" or "Senator Olympia Snowe" to see if that closed the gap.

He probably went even further saying "Senate President Mark Lawrence, the Democrat" or "Senator Olympia Snowe, the Republican." He may even have gone to a truly extensive informed ballot such as giving the respondents a choice between "Senate President Mark Lawrence, the Democrat who has done x, y, and z" or "Senator Olympia Snowe, the Republican who has failed to do x, y, or z."

Thus the challenger will end up with an idea about which characteristics or aspects of achievement the voters want in any given election and what issues separate the challenger from the incumbent in a way that favors the challenger, not the incumbent. It is these issues and these characteristics which the challenger will try to get the voters to identify with him in order to boost his name recognition and his levels of support vis-à-vis the incumbent senator.

Both challengers and incumbents will also have looked closely at the *structure* of the opinion they encountered. The structure is simply the information as to who holds a belief (in this case one for or against a particular candidate) and where are they located, not just in terms of geography (although that can be important in Maine in close races), but also in terms of ethnicity and class.

In order to have a chance even to come close against Olympia Snowe, Lawrence had to make serious inroads in those aspects of the opinion structure that currently favor Senator Snowe. He should have looked long and hard at her huge lead among Franco Americans, those critical swing voters in Maine. He would have to find some issues which move her away from her core of support among women in the home who like her very much. And of course, he had to make major inroads among the more upscale voters of Cumberland County, especially in the towns of Falmouth, Cape Elizabeth, Cumberland, Scarborough, etc. Not an easy task and he failed to accomplish it in the election of 2000!

Of course, to flip the above analysis around and on the smaller playing field of the 1st Congressional District, Jane Amero had the same set of tasks given the structure of Congressman Tom Allen's support. Relying on "Republican" issues or criticism of President Clinton did not help Amero very much except with her Republican base and that, of course, is less than 30 percent of the electorate. Allen scored better with the independent portion of the electorate and she will have to narrow the gap significantly with this cohort if she is to be competitive next fall.

So candidates as well as causes can learn a great deal from the internal aspects of a poll, those that go beyond the simple "head to head" rankings of who is ahead and who is behind. Anybody can see that a particular incumbent is this many points ahead of that challenger. The science comes in determining from the cross tabulations of the demographics (age, sex, income, education, etc.) and psychographics (lifestyles and opinions) where the challenger has advantages and where the incumbent has weaknesses.

The art of politics, of course, comes from turning these polling numbers into reality. In 2000, neither Amero or Lawrence were able to take the initial polling data they uncovered and use it to their electoral advantage. But, looking at it the other way, Congressman Allen and Senator Snowe used their polling data to find out how to keep their challengers at bay for that election cycle.

Campaign Medley

*T*here are a number of items worth considering on the political landscape when we look at the election of 2000, because they have usefulness beyond the specific campaigns of the day.

Last year we had misguided censorship of ads. This time we have censorship of whole campaigns! As I write this, a number of TV stations are ruling out debates saying the outcomes are already known! Can you imagine the hubris of these station wallahs? After all their posturing about the need to get more people to vote? The TV stations ended up having only one combined debate scheduled for the senate race and the two congressionals on PBS, Maine Public Radio, WCSH, and WLBZ.

Sure, the stations had a pretty good idea that all three incumbents would do well and handily defeat their opponents, but they had the audacity to help make these self-fulfilling prophecies by not having enough free airtime for serious debates.

But for goodness sake, we have to have debates. How can the other stations claim to want citizen participation (and bemoan a lack of voter turnout) and yet not have debates? Just think if you gave up six months or a year out of your life to run for public office and just because some station bigwig decided you weren't going to win, he or she canceled the debate.

I think it's pathetic and bad for our democratic process. The stations that don't bother with debates should be ashamed of themselves.

Lost in all the hue and cry about public financing of elections is the hidden truth that many costs of statewide campaigns have gotten relatively less expensive over the last twenty years—think in particular about such items as strategic game plans and telephone costs. And media placement commissions' ad-making fees have stayed relatively flat. By far, the most expensive aspect of any major campaign, the cost of TV time, has risen dramatically over the last twenty years.

In Maine in 2000, to show one commercial at the rate of 1,000 gross rating points (a way of measuring how many people will see your commercial how many times) statewide cost about $125,000. If you figure that each commercial should have 1,000 points behind it in order to be maximally effective and you have five commercials, it will cost you well over a half million dollars in airtime alone.

That is why it is so hypocritical for stations to skip on debates when they have increased and increased their prices year in and year out over the last few decades.

Fourth, I've just finished reading David S. Broder's book, *Democracy Derailed*, sent to me by Jack Havey and Beryl-Ann Johnson of Ad Media.[1] Ad Media has won a lot of ballot measures—as well as the huge upset by Jim Longley Sr. in the 1974 gubernatorial race, and Jack and Beryl-Ann are right to assume this is an important book.

Unfortunately, it's a bad book. I have a lot of respect for David Broder and over the years, I found his columns to be very even-handed and on target and whenever he's talked to me about Maine politics, he seems always to have both protected his sources and fairly represented what they said.

But he clearly doesn't like referenda and *Democracy Derailed* makes a very slanted case against referenda by pushing them to some illogical conclusion as a substitute for representative democracy.

And he's spent a lot of time in California, as if that huge, misbegotten political subsystem could be our guide on much. With the real nuts of the far right and the far left in full hunting cry out there, you get a few excesses. Few sensible people are really suggesting we scrap the Constitution and discard our present system for one that "promises laws without government."[2]

I wish Broder had looked at states like Maine to see what good the referendum process can and does do.

Maine is a much better example about what public initiatives can and do accomplish. The Populists and Progressives who brought us the initiative, were, I believe, correct. The people need a chance to take direct political action when the legislatures (state or national) ignore the people's will for new policies. For example, without the referendum process, we still wouldn't be able to shop on Sunday in the big stores. "Sunday Sales" would still be bottled up in the legislature.

But money is not always the independent variable anyway, certainly not in Maine. Often more money is spent in a losing cause. Think of these examples from recent Maine political history:

1. The side with the most money lost the Bottle Bill contest in 1979.
2. The side with the most money lost the Maine Turnpike widening fight in 1991.
3. The side with the most money lost the Forest Compact I fight in 1996.
4. The side with the most money lost the Forest Compact II fight in 1997.
5. The side with the most money lost the Telephone Measured Service struggle in 1986.
6. The side with the most money lost the Gay Rights II struggle in 1998.

Moreover, Maine people have voted for many, many things over the last fifty years that a majority of us would agree was a good thing. The fact that considerable money needed to be spent in order to keep Public Television on the air (1999), save Bigalow Mountain (1977), pass the $30 million Land Bond (1984), and the $50 million Land Bond (1999) doesn't trouble me and shouldn't trouble Broder.

The problem also is that simple—even simple minded—ideas often require a lot of debate and a lot of money to get across the message that they are wrong for that time and place. I remember especially the Elected Public Utilities Commission struggle of 1981. A state legislator, Bruce Reeves, came up with the idea of an elected PUC and that idea had a lot of appeal on the surface. In fact, 70 percent of Maine voters agreed with that basic concept.

Dick Jalkut, then vice president of New England Telephone came to me and wanted a poll done to see if the Reeves proposal could be defeated. I argued that actually, it might be a good thing to let it pass and then the PUC, like the regulators in Texas, would have to run campaigns. In an elected PUC scenario, the utilities would actually have much more power to elect PUC members more congenial to their causes and understanding of the real issues. Besides, it would have been such fun to chuck Peter Bradford out on his ear! And I didn't think Bruce Reeves would have won a PUC seat in any case.

But Jalkut insisted he wanted to defeat Reeves at the referendum level. The initial polling showed 70 percent for the idea, 20 percent against it, and 10 percent undecided. But the bill itself contained many strange provisions, giving the PUC a lot of power to do things Maine people did not like as much. Once the people learned what was actually in the proposal, support fell away rapidly and once everybody learned what was actually in the bill, it would be defeated 60 percent to 40 percent.

One of these bizarre ideas was a provision that the PUC could go and make treaties with foreign countries! At the time, some in the environmental movement were all excited about Hydro Quebec and bringing all that "cheap and renewable and reliable" energy to Maine. Of course, later, when Hydro Quebec actually came on line, these same experts vigorously objected to the power lines that would bring the energy. Odd they only thought of that later for, to the best of my knowledge, most electricity has always been carried from plants through wires.

I'll grant you one had to spend serious money to defeat this strange idea, but I defy anyone to find many pockets of regret that it was defeated.

Same thing happened in 2000, with Jonathan Carter's Question 2. It was an amazing, off-the-wall set of provisions supposedly designed to "improve" the forest. As a small wood lot owner and long-time participant in the Tree Growth Conservation Program myself, I was reminded of that legendary American captain who, looking at the smoking ruins of the village in Vietnam, said we "had to destroy the village in order to save it."

Carter's half-baked scheme reminded me of that. He would have had us adopt policies that would destroy the forest as we know it, all under the guise of "saving" it. Under his plan, Tree Growth participants would have had to cut the average growth on their property every year or lose the rights to that growth.

Just think of the thousands and thousands of miles of *new* logging roads that would have had to be opened as necessary to comply with his provisions that eight different species have to be harvested every single year on your woodlot or you lose the cutting rights to them. You'd have had to have many, many access roads to the four corners of your property because—at least the last time I looked—nothing in nature forced your eight species to all live in their proper places with easy access. So, since you would have had to cut from their little stands every single year, you need to be able to get to each and every stand of them each and every single year. That's just what we need in Maine, thousands and thousands of miles of new logging roads all over the state. A truly bad idea!

Carter's proposals eventually went down to savage defeat, losing in every county and indeed every town in the state. It was a bad idea yet it took a long time and a lot of effort to defeat it. Even then 28 percent of the electorate cast ballots for it while 72 percent voted against it.

NOTES

1. David S. Broder, *Democracy Derailed* (New York: Harcourt, 2000).
2. Broder, *Democracy Derailed*, p. 243.

The Kiss

$\mathcal{Y}$ou had to see it, I guess, to believe it. I was acting very unprofessional and cavalier during the night Al Gore spoke to the Democratic convention. I was watching a Red Sox game in the workout room, having overdosed on the second generation of "left-wing deviation" as Lenin (and for all that, Trotsky as well) would have called it in a less kind, less gentle age. Can anyone tell me why the Cuomo and Jackson kids couldn't rebel just a bit like everybody else's? To listen to them give the same tired rhetoric as their fathers gave twenty, even thirty years ago, was sad and saddening. Boring too.

So I almost missed it. I came back into the den and thought my wife was watching the Playboy Channel again. This large dude was grabbing this woman, somewhat awkwardly I thought, and kissing her like there was no tomorrow. I mean a real, deep, throat-probing kiss of a kiss. I hadn't seen anything like that since we were riding on the school bus in 1954 and Raymond Greenwood planted a lip lock on Jeanne Vaulker (who bore a startling resemblance to present day Janeane Garofalo) for the better part of ten minutes while everybody on the bus cheered.

For those of you who never saw him on the Nashville Network later on, Raymond was a country boy who lived in Niantic, Connecticut and played the guitar ("just like ringing a bell"). Raymond was also quite the important guy when we were growing up. He'd come from the backwoods of Tennessee or North Carolina at an early age and he was the only kid I knew then who trapped wild animals for fun and profit. He was always bringing pelts of little animals like muskrats onto the school bus. He knew a lot about the forest critters and even made up his own scents that he also brought on the bus. Fox urine was one of the staples as I remember.

One day he brought along a special vial of mixed skunk scent and fox urine. Brought it in a small glass bottle and when the school bus went down a big hill in the next town, he rolled it the length of the bus and it broke, as he intended, under the bus driver's seat. Well, I want you to know that bus driver was some kind of wimp because in a matter of seconds, he yanked the bus over to the side of the road, nearly turning us over. He then jumped out of the bus and said, "You kids want to stink up my bus? You drive it." And he marched down the road and left us right there.

Now by today's standards, the whole thing wasn't much of a transgression. After all, Raymond didn't bring a bear trap to school and set it in the lunchroom. And he never brought an Uzi either (although his moonshine-making clan may well have had a Tommy gun or two lying around). But by the lights of 1954, this was one big deal. Thirty kids standing by the road yelling at the passing cars for forty-five minutes, principal alerted, police called, new bus sent, original driver taken away in an ambulance with oxygen, thought to be having a heart attack or nervous breakdown, kids an hour late for school. It was great.

And didn't we love the interrogation. We were all brought individually down to the principal's office (even the girls who said they didn't like backwoods boys anyway) and grilled; but nobody told on Raymond. Of course, he'd had the foresight to have us all walk in the stuff on the way out of the bus so we all smelled like him and could have been in on the prank.

I remember being singled out as a possible conspirator: "Potholm, you're an instigator and you're known to trap with Raymond." Well, that wasn't quite right. Raymond had gotten me to set out one trap one night in a pond near my house with a raw carrot as bait. I'd woken up at 4 AM the next morning, all excited to get out there and check my "trap line" before school. But all I caught was one water rat which Raymond admitted wasn't worth the trouble, even for him. "You can't even eat them," he said. That was the end of my Daniel Boone phase. The principal did get quite angry when I told him I had hay fever and couldn't smell anything.

But nobody told and no one was ever punished, except of course the bus driver for ratting us out. When he returned to drive us that winter, we locked him out of the bus in the freezing cold on one of the stops when he went outside to see what all the other drivers were pointing at. It was the mechanical "Stop" sign which Raymond kept pushing out with his foot from his new vantage point right behind the bus driver where the driver thought he could keep his eye on Raymond. He couldn't, of course.

Now I know this is going to sound crazy in this yuppified age but Raymond had quite a cachet with the girls even though, as I say, he made his own scents and often smelled like a whole pack of wild animals. So when the girls on the bus decided to "break the kissing record," he was selected. He, like Gore, looked a little awkward getting his arms around Jeanne at the beginning, but once he got going, he wouldn't let her up for air. Again, like Al. And Jeanne, like Tipper, thought this was about the coolest thing she'd ever been a part of and she got into it as well. Flapping her little arms but keeping the kiss going. Again, just like Tipper.

Like a lot of people watching Al and Tipper last month, my reaction was mixed. On the one hand, it was a bit embarrassing to watch that initial awkwardness (no Sean Connery he) but once the embrace got going, you had to cheer for Al. After all, he's had eight years of hearing what a randy stud his boss was and now he had his chance in front of sixty million people (including some delegates who have only a dim recollection of Woodstock) to show his stuff. I'd say he made the most of it. What a studmuffin! And with his own wife. I'll bet a lot of Viagra was used that night by many of the delegates and viewers. "If he can do it. . . ."

And just why is this of any relevance? Because I'm a pollster, that's why, and anything like a 17-point swing in national polling deserves our close attention—at least for a moment. Or at least until *People* magazine gives us the inside story. This "convention bounce" theory is a tad weak in spots, but you can't deny that before "The Kiss," W. was ahead by quite a bit and after "The Kiss," he was behind by quite a bit.

Now I'm sure there's more to the bounce than "The Kiss" (although probably not much more). We party regulars get all caught up in the inside baseball stuff but I guess to many Americans watching the

Democratic convention, it was now possible to turn to one's spouse or significant other and say "Did you see that honey? Why he *is* alive after all."

But, I think there is another side to all this. I always believe that one candidate can't account for such a big swing all by his or her lonesome. It takes two to tango and usually there is something of a mirror image with one candidate doing some things right and another doing things wrong which, when you fit them together, accounts for the polling movement. In other words, it's hard to make up ground when your opponent is doing well too.

The answer in this case, may simply lie in that mirror image. What were the Republican pundits so excited about during W.'s convention? First, they were happy for a few minority faces. Second, they were happy there was no huge fight about abortion. Or the vice-presidential pick. Talk about boring (and a mistake)! Third, the real right-wing speakers were nestled safe and sound and secure at the podium in time frames opposite the soaps. Fourth, there was some good sticking it to the old D's with the images they regard as their own. I personally liked the strong rhetoric by some minority speakers. I know Condoleezza Rice blew me away with her story about her father having to register as a Republican in the South of the 1950s because the Democrats wouldn't enroll him. Not much of a follow up by the national press on that story but it was a nice juxtaposition!

But beyond these pluses, the Republican pundits were so overjoyed that W. got through the whole convention without a smirk. That's right. I heard three or four of them complimenting W. and his brain trust for pulling off the whole convention without a single smirk. "He didn't smirk once," said a serious looking fellow, "that's progress."

I don't know. Now, I obviously can't speak either for women or for men who like men—although I can say I personally would take Laura ahead of Tipper were I taking somebody to the prom in 1958 and those were the choices.

But with those qualifiers, I think that W.'s smirk is kind of sexy.

Not overpoweringly sexy, no; but sexy nevertheless. Think of Marlon Brando. Or James Dean. My poor mother cried when I put him in my high school yearbook as "my idol" instead of her suggestion, Albert Schweitzer. Mom, I know you are up in heaven and I know now you were right, at least about James. Or take Elvis. Elvis was hips and a smirk. Well maybe bedroom eyes, hips, and a smirk, but he had a real humdinger of a smirk.

No, when they took the smirk away from W., they took away a lot of his charm. Remember, he'd closed the Republican gender gap with the smirk in place. Taking away the smirk and its charm just as Gore was really letting loose with "The Kiss" really had a cumulative effect on the body politic. It had a big multiplier effect. Hopefully for W., a transitory one, but the overnights seldom lie for that night's polling snapshot. Something happened and it weren't all good! Let W. be W. again! Turn that tiger loose!

Can you believe this? The second most populous democracy in the world (think "India") and we are reducing the presidential contest to smirks and kisses. Believe me, it isn't just me either. Everybody was talking about "The Kiss" the next day, pundits, commentators, spinners, reporters. *Today, Good Morning America,* and *The Early Show* all featured it as a huge story. Matt Lauer even led off the *Today* show with a question to Al about it. And wasn't Al some pleased! He lit up like a Christmas tree. Days later, *USA Today* had a headline on the front page which read "Gore, Under Questioning, Insists the Kiss Was Just a Kiss." The story would not die. A week later the *Wall Street Journal* reported "Gore Gaining Ground . . . Partly Due to Convention Kiss." Are you kidding me?

This was big time news! Let's face it, TV is about emotion and image and giving the audience something to think about and "The Kiss" sure did that.

It may sound like we're trivializing this election. But what the hell, if it sells, bottle it and as Raymond Greenwood always told me, even if it doesn't sell right now, keep a bottle of it around, you never know when you will have an occasion to use it. For something.

Round One to Gore.

Who's going to moderate these presidential debates anyway?

I just had a great idea. Invite all the candidates.

Have the candidates' wives (not their vice presidents) stand behind their men, kissing them when they do well and turning their lips away pointedly when the lads make a mistake? Tipper and Al, Laura and W., Shelley Ann and Pat. Ralph? Pat can lend him his sister, Bay. Ralph and Bay. Now there's a match truly made in political heaven. I've never seen her smile either.

I'd pay to watch that kind of debate, even if the Red Sox are still in the wildcard hunt. I already know how their quest is going to turn out.

Same way it always does.

This other race?

It's going to be worth watching.

POSTSCRIPT

And it certainly was!

Part IV

LEADERSHIP IN DEMOCRACY

An Ode to Chuck

The death of Alton E. "Chuck" Cianchette leaves Maine a poorer place.

Maine politics is full of wonderful people dedicated to making the state a better place and living their lives as inspiration for the rest of us.

Chuck Cianchette was such a person and more. He was very special. Everyone who met Chuck was better off for his smile and his caring and his living examples of giving, sharing, and making things better.

A gentle, loving, kind giant with a huge heart, Chuck always led by example. His philanthropy is well known and widely documented. He worked tirelessly for such organizations as the Boy Scouts, Maine Central Institute, and the Susan L. Curtis Foundation. He gave of his time, and his money, his inspiration, and his drive, and organizational ability. He was strong in his family and his faith and especially strong in his knowledge of what his company, Cianbro, could do only with the help of its workers. He was probably the most "secure" person I've ever met, for he fitted his time, his family, his business, and his state with ease and grace.

Chuck's influence on Maine politics was all out of proportion to the several terms he served in the Maine Senate in the 1970s and again later in the 1990s. Before, during, and after his formal participation in Maine legislative politics, Chuck often worked behind the scenes with members of both parties to make life better for people in Maine.

He put Maine first, then his party. He donated much money and much effort to many Democratic candidates, but he was truly nonpartisan in his vision and his outlook. He would work with anyone who was seeking to make Maine a better place.

A conservative Democrat, he would have made an ideal governor, concerned about the welfare of others but committed to making Maine a good place to conduct business and thereby raise the standard of living for others. Yet he was realistic enough to know that the liberal wing of his party would never accept a pro-development businessman as their standard-bearer.

Unlike many in politics, Chuck was always very aboveboard and straightforward. I remember quite clearly toward the end of John Martin's Speakership when many cursed him and wished he would be removed. Many disliked John's style of leadership, many disliked his policies, and many would plot and scheme behind his back. But most were simply afraid of him, his power, and his willingness to use that power to get even in some way.

Once he decided that Martin had to be removed, however, Chuck Cianchette had the guts to fly his plane up to Eagle Lake and tell John to his face that for the good of the party and the good of the state, he would have to go. And that if he did not resign gracefully, Chuck would lead the effort to oust him.

This was a remarkable mission for a remarkable man and yet, when I encountered Chuck much later on the very day Martin resigned, I did not see joy or gloating or self-satisfaction. I thought he would be delighted to have accomplished his stated purpose and told him so. Chuck simply replied, "John's a good man, he'll learn his lesson from this and come back; he has a lot to offer yet."

That incident tells you a lot about the kind of man Chuck was: a straight shooter, a stand up guy, someone who didn't shy away from a challenge or conflict but looked his opponent right in the eye while meeting that challenge and told him or her exactly what he was going to do; someone who didn't believe in grudges; someone who believed that when the battle—whatever it was—was over, he wanted to shake hands and bury the hatchet and move on. And, no small thing in this cynical age, Chuck always believed in redemption, political and otherwise.

Some of his causes succeeded (most notably worker's compensation reforms) and some have yet to come to pass (the East–West

Highway and meaningful tort reform), but in the pursuit of all of them, Chuck showed class and character and a wonderful sense of fair play. He had a marvelous sense of humor and could always laugh at his own shortcomings. He didn't think in terms of enemies, only temporary adversaries. His joy in life was contagious.

As president of Cianbro Corporation, he made safety "almost a religion." It was, he said, the workers that made the company what it was and it was they who would suffer if safety was not paramount. He was legendary for sharing rewards for jobs done well and on time with his crew.

Through all of his political activities, Chuck exhibited what Jay Hardy called "The serenity of Buddha," a calming aura which was contagious to all around him. In politics, when the going gets tough, usually the tough go into a hissy fit. But Chuck could almost always calm things down and get people who were riled up to focus on the important issue at hand and to channel their nervous energy into something productive.

Chuck, of course, was not *always* Buddha-like or a saint. There is the classic tale of his meeting with the board of the Natural Resources Council of Maine. As chairman of the Environmental and Economic Council of Maine, a group seeking balance between environmental and development concerns, Chuck thought that the NRCM went way too far in its concerns over "parts per billion" of dioxin.

Exasperated at their continual intransigence, Chuck stood in front of the board and offered to "eat a brick of asbestos and drink a gallon of dioxin" right there and then. No one on the flummoxed board wanted to take him up on it.

I had the good fortune to spend a fair amount of time with Chuck on various campaign trails, plotting and planning, seeking to actualize goals in the political arena, and he was always the same: quick to give credit to others when something worked, and just as quick to take full responsibility when something did not.

Chuck was also the first to see the best in people and to overlook their faults. He gave everyone the benefit of the doubt and even when disappointed in someone, he always gave them another chance to prove themselves.

In one of his 1990 reelection bids for the Maine Senate, organized labor went to great lengths to find him an opponent and put a lot of muscle behind her efforts in the Democratic primary. Chuck took the challenge good-naturedly but seriously and when the race got close, he got up at 5:00 AM and pressed the flesh in diners and country stores all over his district, turning aside the challenge with old fashioned hard work and a very loyal family, employees, and campaign staff. He did not take his status or wealth or previous accomplishments for granted. He went out and proved himself again. That's the kind of man he was.

Maine has lost a great and noble son.

A Life of Courage

$\mathcal{I}$n May 2000, Charles William Petersen of Portland died after a truly heroic battle with cancer. He was known as "Talle" to many of his friends, and "Doc" to the teachers and students of Edward Little High School where he taught history and military studies for many years. He was beloved by many for his dedication to his students, his craft, and to his school. Several hundred students and teachers attended his recent funeral for he had given a lifetime of service to the community.

Although Charlie was my cousin, he was more like a brother to me. He was a year older and lived in Portland when I was growing up in Connecticut. He and his family came down to Long Island Sound for the summer so we saw a lot of each other and we also came every other year to Portland for Christmas. He introduced me to Maine, LL Bean, and history, especially military history, World War II, and the joys of police work. After we both graduated from Bowdoin, we worked five summers together as policemen in Old Lyme, Connecticut where we were joined by the rookie cop Bill Cohen. Bill Cohen doing police work with a .357 Magnum and a small red sports car is still talked about on the Connecticut shore! After graduating from Deering High in 1957, Charlie went into the army and served two years in Germany where he was a Military Policeman (MP). When he got out, he headed for Bowdoin, one year behind Bill and me.

But his life was not easy after that. The day he arrived at Bowdoin, his father died and he ended up commuting to classes from his home on Baxter Boulevard in Portland. With his father gone so suddenly, there was no money for college and he relied on scholarships and working every day to pay the bills. As soon as classes were over, he went to work in a shoe factory in Ft. Andros, Brunswick before finally heading back to Portland for the night. Then just when he was adjusted to college life, during his junior year at Bowdoin, he was diagnosed with testicular cancer and underwent a major operation and massive doses of radiation and chemotherapy.

Despite all this, Charlie graduated with highest honors in history from Bowdoin and went on to get his Ph.D. in military history. While at Bowdoin, he met and later married his wife Marlene and adopted her four children. He was just beginning to get his feet on the ground, teaching at Wilton High School in Connecticut when he was again stricken with cancer and underwent a second major operation on his other side and the same massive doses of radiation and chemotherapy. This bout left him permanently crippled by massive fluid buildup in his legs.

Yet Charlie soldiered on all these years, coming back to Maine to teach at Edward Little where he became the chair of his department and guided several generations of students on to college and the military. He was one of those rare teachers who lead by example and he worked equally well with those college bound and those just counting the days until high school was over. Finally last fall, he was stricken again, losing fifty or sixty pounds in a few months. But he remained teaching as long as he could even sit up in the classroom and went to the hospital only under duress and the insistence of his family. He died after several operations.

When he finally succumbed, the outpouring of grief from his friends, students, and faculty was a fitting tribute to his life and his courage. Frankly, I have never met anyone more courageous. His courage was truly incredible. In the almost sixty years I knew him, I never—ever—heard him complain or bemoan his fate. Most people I know, myself included, would have complained about the hand we had been dealt. Not Charlie. He never used his medical history to help him along. He just soldiered on, asking for no favors and expecting none. In fact, growing up, he often kidded me that our family spent more on colds than his did on cancer.

He always had a cherry and kind word for everybody and always looked on the bright side of things no matter what the circumstances.

He was really one tough guy. A couple of summers ago, I took him blue fishing and he hooked a good sized one only to have a harbor seal come along and take the fish in his mouth. There we were, going down the bay pulled by a seal that had decided to keep the blue. Charlie yanked and yanked on the line and the treble hook finally came out of the fish. Out of the fish, but a second later, into Charlie's leg. There he was with two of the three hooks imbedded in his leg. "Boy, we'd better get you back" I said, but he shook his head. "I'm all right," he said. "Let's stay and catch some blues." Three hours later we sat in the emergency room as the doctor said, not too politely, "How long has this been in your leg?" The picture of Charlie holding up two blues with the hook in his leg was his Christmas card for that holiday season.

For many years, he and his wife Marlene were also well known on the Republican political trail. Marlene became a political operative in her own right, running for the Maine House in a largely Democratic district and coming quite close to victory. For many years, they were party stalwarts who supported Republican candidates whenever they could.

Both Charles and Marlene were more than just individuals who followed Maine politics. They both represent the small—and dwindling—number of party supporters who are the true activists on the Maine political scene. Too often we overlook their contributions to the political process, focusing on the candidates, their media firms, pollsters, and other high priced consultants associated with campaigns. But it is often the little known workers who provide the foot soldiers for campaigns. They show up at airport and downtown rallies. They speak out for their candidates and their causes.

Their tasks are legion. They get out and put up signs at election time. They work stuffing envelopes and help organize volunteers. They go door to door distributing leaflets. They man phone banks. They copy telephone numbers down on voter lists. They keep up the spirits of the candidates, often cheering them when no one else will. They serve on the city, town, county, and state committees for their parties.

Sometime they are paid, especially if they work as field personnel, traveling from one end of the state to the other. But most often they are not. They do their political activity because they like it and consider it their civic duty. They like being a part of the Maine political scene and having a say in how things turn out at election time. They follow the political process closely, knowing who the players are and what are the issues that interest people. They are always listening to what others say and bring important information to candidates and their staff. They are the foot soldiers in the small armies that make up political campaigns, be they candidate or ballot measure.

Over the last twenty years, I have worked with the Petersens in a number of political focus groups. With uncanny accuracy, they participated by representing not only their own views but those of a large percentage of the Republican and Independent cohorts in Maine. For example, I remember doing a focus group in Lewiston when Mike Dukakis was 17 percent ahead of George Bush and Charlie Petersen brought all the reasons Dukakis would eventually lose. After the focus group, the liberal group paying for the focus group kept referring to Charlie as "that Fascist who was unfair to Mike," but he was proven very correct when election night finally came.

Lifelong Republicans, Charlie and Marlene started out as activists in party politics with Bill Cohen and his campaign for Congress in 1972. They supported him early in the Republican primary that year when Cohen defeated the better known and more experienced Abbot Green. The Petersens came on board early and worked tirelessly as volunteers for Cohen and in the summer of 1972, I chose them to be field personnel for Oxford and Androscoggin counties, the two most important counties in our game plan. Normally Republican candidates had been coming out of the Androscoggin valley down 23,000 votes. Bill Cohen was to lose the two by only 6,000.

Thus the Petersens were with Cohen the first day when he began his 600-mile walk across the state from Gilead to Ft. Kent. I have always been amused that Bill Cohen, now Secretary of Defense and now leader of several million service men and women, started out with such a small band of followers. The first day of the walk certainly tried the patience of the candidate and those accompanying him. Charles and Marlene walked with Bill that very first day which was almost the last day of the effort.

That first day was horrible.

It was hot and still as only rural Maine can be hot and still in July.

The candidate had yet to hit his stride navigating the shoulders of rural roads and had several narrow escapes from speeding cars.

And oh, what cars. There were streams and streams of them. Often the traffic was bumper to bumper in long lines coming from north to south. Initially I was very excited about the traffic flow and all the people who were driving by and waving wildly. Excited that is until Charlie and Marlene pointed out that most of the cars had Canadian plates; they were visitors from Quebec, headed for the Maine coast and Old Orchard Beach and no matter how alluring that destination, not likely to still be in Maine come November.

"Not many voters here," said the candidate ruefully.

On and on we trudged, sweltering, frustrated, and very soon, very sore and very tired. Even then Charlie's body had been weakened by his first and second bouts with cancer and the concomitant radiation and chemotherapy. But as the rest of us complained, Charlie strode on, never complaining, never asking for a break.

Bill and I were both challenged by his perseverance.

Charles William Petersen: a true profile in courage.

Millennium Credit

$\mathcal{A}$s America stands at the beginning of the twenty-first century, it is more than a little amazing and quite ironic how we got where we are. Those of us who follow politics are likely to either wildly exaggerate or considerably undervalue the role our leaders play, especially our presidents. Yet some reflections seem in order.

William Jefferson Clinton came to office after twelve years of Republican executive control. To many Democrats he was the Second Coming of John F. Kennedy, a "New Democrat" who would wipe away the sins of the Republican past and lead his party to a new dawn of opportunity and social engineering.

A month before his inauguration, I gave a talk to the Brunswick Town and Gown club in which I pointed out that Clinton's demonstrated forte was not governing but campaigning and that he and the people closest to him lived for the campaign moment with its war room, the sense of time being speeded up by events, and a world of enemies, real and imagined. I called him the "Robo Candidate" for his ability to shrug off incredible political shots and take hits which would doom most other political figures. I also pointed out that he utterly lacked any moral compass and would do anything and say anything to stay "in the game."

This was one of those rare occurrences where you know absolutely and utterly you are right, that you have correctly predicted events and processes which will come to pass and yet the audience is totally, unalterably opposed to what you have to say. My remarks were greeted by

113

the largely Democratic audience with disbelief, overt hostility, and something close to derision. But then, my opening line, delivered in December 1992—"It is probably too early to speak of the failed presidency of Bill Clinton"—may have unnecessarily put them off their feed. Sometimes we professors like to be provocative just to get our audience's attention.

As the first year of the Clinton presidency unfolded, the clumsiness, the lack of loyalty, the missteps, the ideologically driven health care fight and the perpetual campaign atmosphere were there for all to see. It was a circus.

And yet looking back today, I believe Clinton not only turned out to be a very good president, he turned out to be a very good Republican president. Think if you will where we are today. The stock market is at an all time high. Inflation is the lowest in fifty years. The budget is balanced! Interest rates are down. Unemployment is its lowest in thirty years. Millions of people are off the welfare rolls for the first time in generations. There are 100,000 more police officers on the streets. There are more criminals behind bars than ever before in our country's history. Edwin Meese and the shade of Richard Nixon are happy.

The philosophy of free trade rules much of our national government's thinking. Trillions and trillions of dollars of new wealth have been created as technology and the Internet transform our lives daily and entrepreneurship is at an all time high as IPOs surge daily, creating new opportunities and the venture capital to try thousands of new ideas. Most Americans are far better off than they were seven years ago and their retirement accounts prove it.

If we didn't know who had been in the White House while all this was going on, wouldn't we assume it was a Republican administration?

Of course, Republicans have played an important role in keeping Clinton aiming toward these goals. The Republican Congress has in fact been most frustrated by the fact that Clinton has taken most of their good ideas and made them his own.

You have only to read the insider accounts of the Clinton administration by Robert Reich and George Stephanopoulos to appreciate their frustration at Clinton becoming a de facto Republican. Reich, as Secretary of Labor, was stunned to discover that Alan Greenspan, the head of the Federal Reserve, and Robert Rubin, the Wall Street banker, were in fact making economic policy for the Clinton administration and what's more, Clinton liked it that way! Stephanopoulos' "growing disillusionment," corresponded to his being outmaneuvered in the on-going "campaign" by Dick Morris, the Republican strategist.

Of course Morris continues to be his own strategist, not caring a fig for the Republicans, Democrats, or anybody else. But it was his genius to come to Clinton with the notion of "triangulation," a fancy term for "stealing the other guy's ideas" and thus positioning yourself in an unassailable position in the middle of the political spectrum.

And it was Clinton's genius to see in "triangulation" as a perpetual campaign tactic, a way to make governing fun, more like a campaign and less like government as taught in civics classes. He would never "lose" if he took all the Republican ideas and made them his own, even as he kept all the Democratic ideas and beat the Republicans over the head with them.

There is a marvelous passage in Morris' book in which Clinton, bored out of his mind during a foreign policy meeting on Bosnia, calls Morris and asks him detailed questions about how the polling shows he's doing in New York! Triangulation turned out to be a way to always be in campaign mode while appearing to be in policy mode.

Clinton thrived on it and left the national Republicans sitting in the dust, confused, frustrated, and irritated with the American people who refused to take their eyes off the economic and social ball to follow the moral ball as Clinton continued to show himself shall we say—not to put too fine a point on it—sexually pathetic.

Yet today, how many readers even have any idea who the Republican leaders are in the House or Senate, let alone what they stand for. Who cares? Clinton has demolished them all and taken their ideas and made them his own. Newt who?

So let's give credit where credit is due. America in 2002 is better off for having experienced the Clinton presidency. He could have presided over an altogether different administration. Everybody knows that Democrats are basically best at spending other people's money and creating bureaucracies to be staffed by their sons and daughters in order to try to solve insoluble problems and look busy while failing. Yes, I know Republicans are best at trying to keep all the money they make and not caring much about other people, but that's a subject for another chapter.

Clinton could have gone the liberal Johnson route or the Jimmy Carter dilettante route, but he did not. He alienated the left wing of his own party (a very good thing for the country) and took all the popular ideas of the right and made them into reality (also a very good thing for the country). He didn't make the myriad of economic and legislative policy mistakes that would have killed the goose of economic prosperity he inherited. We shouldn't give Clinton too much credit for the current economic state of affairs, but we shouldn't give him too little either. As Americans, we often don't give our leaders credit for letting things alone. Clinton left the economy alone.

And while we're on the subject of giving credit where credit is due, how about a little praise for the guy who started it all? Ronald Reagan remains one of our most important post–World War II presidents. Like a Norman Rockwell painting, his surface simplicity and superficiality mask a much deeper and more authentic reality.

Objective historians in the twenty-first century will reevaluate his presidency and speak of it in glowing terms. He said with the clarity of a Winston Churchill that the Soviet Union was an "evil empire." It was, of course, slaughtering millions of its own people and enslaving millions of other peoples. Reagan declared, as no American president had, that not only was communism a failed system, it had to be rolled back. He also set about doing just that.

He said to the military: spend all the money you need. Make us first in everything. Engage the Soviets on all levels and on all fronts. Most people have now forgotten the world Reagan inherited from Jimmy Carter. America a pathetic, blundering giant, demoralized and defeated in Vietnam, on the defensive in Nicaragua, Angola, and Afghanistan, America at the mercy of Iran—for God's sake—and unable to coordinate a six helicopter rescue mission.

Reagan gave America back its pride and its military might and showed in Libya, Panama, Grenada, and the Middle East that we were not afraid to use it. Reagan showed truly courageous leadership to win the Cold War. He let loose the CIA to combat the Soviets across the globe. He went on the offensive and said what had to be said: "Tear down this Wall." Best of all, he latched onto the Strategic Defense Initiative (SDI), often called Star Wars. He saw that as an irrefutable advantage the United States could have and having it, could bankrupt the Soviet Union.

Lost in all the political posturing in the debate over SDI (including whether it could ever work or not) was the simple logic it entailed. Without SDI, the Soviets had the ability to hit the United States with 6,000 nuclear weapons. With SDI, they would have needed 300,000 nuclear weapons to do the same thing. Moreover, they could not afford to act as if SDI didn't work. Even if it only worked a little bit, their strategic nuclear task would be overwhelming.

Recent disclosures from the Soviet archives show that the Soviet leadership feared SDI more than any other potential weapon and it was Reagan who most steadfastly refused to give it up until the Cold War was over. SDI may have been a simple idea, but it was a very powerful one and Reagan believed in it and thus made the Soviets believe in it too.

The Soviet Union disintegrated because (1) it was an evil empire and evil empires are hard to sustain over time, (2) communism is a stupid economic system which could not compete over time with a strong market system, and (3) the United States under Reagan pushed back hard against it on all fronts using our tremendous advantage of a market economy. Yes, Reagan almost bankrupted our economy paying for our unprecedented military buildup and tax cuts, but he *did* bankrupt the Soviet economy.

Reagan pushed through tax cuts, including a vital reduction in the capital gains tax (which, at 50 percent, was a significant barrier to economic development), thus setting the stage for the greatest and longest economic boom in American history. He also appointed Alan Greenspan to head the Federal Reserve to make sure inflation was brought under control.

So Reagan should get lots of credit for starting us on the path of economic, military, and political revival and Clinton should get credit for sustaining our resurgence.

Top Ten

$\mathscr{A}$s we begin the twenty-first century, there are more and more top ten lists of everything from weather highlights to national movie stars. It is often fun to look back and sum up. In this spirit, I am presenting who I take to be the top ten political figures who have had the most fundamental impact on the Maine political scene since World War II.

Who stands out from the last fifty years of Maine politics?

Who did the most to make the Maine political system what it is at the end of this century?

As I present this list, please be advised that I am only including those figures who I believe have had a major impact on the *Maine* political system. I am deliberately leaving out a number of prominent Maine political figures—such as Fred Payne or George Mitchell—who have played important roles on the *American* political scene without having as great an impact on the ongoing Maine political scene. For a fuller exploration of many of the themes, see my *An Insider's Guide to Maine Politics*[1] available from Amazon.com.

In reverse order, the top ten are:

10. *Harrison "Harry" Richardson*—A very influential Republican state representative and senator from Cumberland, who, as majority leader in the House during the Curtis years (1966–1974), helped establish the modern state government of Maine. The state income tax, the basic environmental protection acts, educational funding, and the statewide education

system all came about with his help and that of other moderate Republicans (such as Dick Hewes, Joe Sewall, Rosy Susi, Ken McCloud, and Ben Katz) who worked with Governor Curtis to make the Maine state government what it is today. How much of a magician was Harry the Horse? He got the income tax through without a public hearing!

9. *Dave Emery/Joe Brennan*—This unlikely and almost-never-linked duo actually had a most profound impact on Democratic politics, keeping the liberal wing of the Democratic Party in the First District from attaining political office for over twenty years. Between the two of them, they kept several entire generations of young Democrats at bay, defeating them in primaries or general elections and otherwise blocking their upward mobility.

Together, Emery and Brennan scythed down twenty-eight Democratic challengers in primaries and general elections and had a major impact on a twenty-year Democratic cohort, one which includes the likes of Peter Kyros, Barry Hobbins, Dick Spencer, Rick Barton, Phil Merrill, Sandy Maisel, Hal Pachios, Spike Carey, Sean Faircloth, and many others. Not until the later successes of Tom Andrews and Tom Allen did the liberal wing of the Democratic Party get to stake out the First District seat as its own.

8. *Olympia Snowe/Jock McKernan*—She won more major elections since World War II than any other political figure in Maine. Unbeaten in nine major races, Olympia Snowe set the electoral standard by which all must henceforth be judged. Jock was 6 and 0 himself. Both Snowe and McKernan have consistently been undervalued as campaign strategists, but their enduring legacy is one of a combined win total of fifteen elections won and none lost. There is a lot of skill involved in running up such a record. Some luck, true, but a lot more skill.

7. *John Martin*—The (then) youngest person ever elected to the Maine legislature and the longest serving Speaker of the House. Brought into the Maine political system by the Ed Muskie–Frank Coffin revolution, he always cared deeply for those then out of power and out of favor—the elderly, the poor, especially the rural poor, those in Aroostok county, and

Franco Americans and others who had been discriminated against.

He completely reformed the legislative process, establishing a permanent staff for the legislature, banning lobbyists from the well of the House, and opening up work sessions of committees to the public. Regarded by some as excessively partisan, he may have missed a few opportunities for greatness but his legacy is still accomplishment enough—and it is not over. In fact, given the current disarray among Democrats in the House, he could emerge as the next Speaker!

6. *Bob Monks*—The modern Republican Party and modern politics with its political techniques which we take for granted (including targeted mailings, continual polling, scientific scheduling, professional campaign management, computer generated thank you notes) either came with Bob Monks or were forcefully interjected into later successful campaigns by other Republicans he assisted.

   In the watershed year of 1972, although Monks lost the Republican primary, he in effect turned overall Republican fortunes around, rejuvenated the party, and actively recruited subsequently successful candidates. Without his help, it is doubtful Bill Cohen, Dave Emery, Jock McKernan, and Olympia Snow would have been as successful as they were.

5. *James "Jim" Longley Sr./Angus King*—Although they are very different in temperament and accomplishments, these two Independent Party governors of Maine, twenty years apart, had considerable impact on the Maine political scene. Combative and showing a continuing dislike for state government, Longley set the stage for a dozen imitators and challenged the orthodoxy of both major political parties. As part of his legacy, twice as many Independents ran in the period 1976 to 1998 than had run from 1940 to 1974 before he provided the example. At the same time, myths aside, Longley did virtually nothing to check the size of state government or state spending, both of which actually increased during his tenure.

   For his part, King actually has reformed state government by insisting the state adopt modern accounting and fiscal policies and more rationally allocate its scarce resources. Maine is now

being run more like a true business. There are now 1,000
fewer state workers than when he came into office, thus making King the first governor since John Reed to have presided
over the shrinking of state government.

Also, welfare rolls are at their lowest since 1969 and the
Rainy Day Fund has gone from $5 million to $135 million,
the largest in the state's history. The number of state workers linked to the Internet has gone from zero to 9,000 and
overall productivity is up sharply as Maine is increasingly
linked to the global economy. Quite a set of accomplishments with three more years to go to the formation of his
legacy.

4. *Governor Kenneth "Ken" Curtis*—Elected by a narrow (3 percent) margin in 1966 and reelected by an even narrower one
(0.1 percent) in 1970 after passage of the state income tax,
Curtis transformed the nature of Maine government. His suc-
cessive administrations made the modern state what it is today with its cabinet system, extensive bureaucratic apparatus
and central planning for education, income redistribution,
and environmental protection concerns.

Exuberant, open, and a true compromiser, Curtis shaped the
character of Maine state government as no one before and
provided the impetus for its growth. In doing so, he re-
sponded to the deep felt needs of Maine people and set in
motion the course of modern government in Maine. Without
realizing the extent of his contributions, current Republicans
and Democrats fight over his legacy every election cycle. His
legacy usually wins.

3. *Margaret Chase Smith*—Independent, feisty, and self-made,
she became the model for subsequent independent and moderate Republican women. Both present senators, Susan
Collins and Olympia Snowe (as well as Bill Cohen), followed
her "independent" stance both on issues and on party loyalty.
Margaret Chase Smith set the pattern, breaking away from
the "Good old boys" who ran the Republican Party from the
Civil War until 1948. By winning the Republican primary for
U.S. Senate in 1948 and doing it "her way" without the tradi-
tional core of political insiders, she set in motion forty years

of Republican candidates who succeeded without that party apparatus.

2. *Bill Cohen*—From 1972 until the present, moderate Republican candidates have dominated the political system of Maine, winning over 60 percent of the major elections. This is due to what I have called the Cohen counterrevolution. Less well known than the Muskie revolution but almost as important on the Maine political scene, this counterrevolution cracked a sixteen-year Democratic grip on the electoral politics of the state.

Although Cohen was not a party builder by temperament or desire, he led by example both attracting new, younger, more moderate Republicans to the political fray and also by having his campaigns serve as models for how to stay in the center of the political spectrum and gather Democratic and Independent support. From 1954 until 1972 Democrats had won the major offices by a 2–1 margin; after Cohen, Republicans went back to 60–40 percent, a ratio they maintained until the end of the twentieth century.

1. *Ed Muskie*—Because of the 1954 to 1972 Muskie Revolution which made the Democrats competitive in Maine for the first time in over a century, I judge him to have been the most influential political figure since World War II. Ed Muskie successfully challenged the Maine political culture which had held sway since before the Civil War and had emphasized business leaders, small business, minimal government, and low tax rates. Muskie also attracted a host of other successful Democrats who eventually came to dominate the Maine political system: Ken Curtis, George Mitchell, Frank Coffin, Bill Hathaway, and Joe Brennan. Muskie made of Maine a genuine two-party state for the first time since before the Civil War.

NOTE

1. Christian P. Potholm, *An Insider's Guide to Maine Politics 1946–1996* (Lanham, Md.: Madison Books, 1998).

Run, Ralphie, Run

I love it!

Ralph Nader is running as a Green! It's so beautiful I can hardly contain myself. Now Ralph has always struck me as Darth Vadar without charm—self satisfied, supercilious, and vain. Or as Pat Buchanan supposedly described him: "Someone with the personality of an East German bureaucrat." Before the fall of the Berlin Wall no doubt!

Frankly, I've always thought about Nader as something of a hypocrite too. For years he demanded that candidates who run for public office disclose their financial holdings but then when he ran for president in 1996 as a Green, he refused to disclose his own! Can you imagine the gall of the man? Of course the craven press corps let him get away with it as is their wont. Then too, Ralph's campaign style in 1996 made McKinley's front porch strategy in 1896 seem like a human dynamo!

What did the Greens get out of him on that go-round? Nothing. Nada. Zip. It made me quite angry!

Truth be told, I've always had a warm spot in my heart for the Greens. My good friend and colleague at Bowdoin, John "Greendaddy" Rensenbrink, was one of the founders of the Green Party in Maine and I do love to talk with him about politics. He always has a fresh way of looking at our political system. In fact, I think he taught Ralph the word "duopoly" —about the Republicans and Democrats being the same. When John ran for the U.S. Senate in 1998 as a Green, I thought he brought stature to the ticket and his campaign was both thoughtful and substantive. He's always represented to me the best of the Greens, raising important issues and getting us to focus on the environment and political system and their interconnection.

And the Greens have done some good work in their time in Maine, helping Angus King to get elected by taking away lots of Brennan votes on Munjoy Hill and the Peninsula in Portland (Brennan's home territory) and making sure Olympia Snowe stayed in Congress on her way to the U.S. Senate.

The Greens are also good at raising important issues. For those interested in this year's official platform as passed by the Greens in Denver, go to www.gp.org. Do not go to www.greenparty.org. as I did initially. Thanks to John, I now know that the web site www.greenparty.org is *not* the official position of the official, Nader-led Greens. Apparently the "left wing radicals," some rump version of the Greens, operates the former site, having grabbed the best name first! To be completely honest, until he told me, I didn't know there *was* a radical left wing of the Greens! I didn't see how there *could* be a radical left wing of the Greens although now I can. I guess Kermit the Frog was right after all when he said "It isn't easy being Green."

But why have Ralphie as a standard bearer in 2000 for the Greens? I'm calling him "Ralphie" from now on instead of "Ralph" because as a good political consultant, I think it makes him sound more loveable. Even though I don't particularly like him, I can't help but give him some sound advice such as going with a perkier name. Ralphie sounds so much more cuddly than "Ralph." And image wise, this not-so-poor lad could use a lot of help. I notice the chaps at his official web site are already working on that front, having dug up somewhere a picture of him smiling instead of scowling. If Ralph's ad agency could elect Jessie Ventura governor, they ought to be able to make Ralph smile and I've already given them his new name gratis.

But if you're a Green, why would you want this guy carrying your banner a second time since he fouled out so ignominiously last time?

Well, I suppose you have to consider whom Ralphie beat out for the nomination this time around. One of his opponents was Jellow Biafra, better known as the lead singer for the Dead Kennedys, and another was Stephen Gaskin, a chap who supposedly runs a commune in Tennessee. In the kingdom of the blind, etc.

Also Nader had the support this time of what he calls "social justice celebrity supporters" (a group Nader would undoubtedly call "fat cats" if they were supporting his opponents!) such as Warren Beatty, Susan Sarandon, and Pearl Jam. At his press conference covered on C-SPAN, Ralph slyly reported that the Vice President had called at least one of these "social justice celebrity supporters" to try to get him or her to support him. No, really. This is a lot of fun!

But back to Nader himself.

I take it this time he promised to campaign at least a little more than last time and before he could get federal matching funds for his campaign, I guess he had to divulge his holdings and conform to the law.

What a nice surprise when he did. It turns out that there may have been a very sensible reason Ralphie didn't file his report in 1996. Although the press has bought and continues to buy the notion that he lives on only $25,000 a year, stays in his sister's apartment in Washington, doesn't own a car, and works only for the people, plowing his speaking fees back into public interest groups, etc. etc. etc., it turns out he's personally been doing quite well.

Quite well indeed.

In fact, according to recent AP accounts, he's a millionaire. That's right, our poor man of the people Ralphie is a millionaire. Well, actually, he's more than a millionaire, he's a multimillionaire! Somehow, the clever little devil has been saving his pennies and not giving them all to the "public interest" groups as everybody thought. The AP puts his net worth at $3.9 million while the *Boston Globe* puts it between $4.09 and $4.96 million! Can you believe these figures?

While ranting and raving all these years against capitalism and corporations, he's amassed a small fortune. Actually it's a big fortune and he's a genuine multimillionaire—a true beneficiary of the capitalist system he derides. I must say that this is a bit like discovering Lenin had two thousand serfs working for him on his estate in the Ukraine while he was having a high old time in Switzerland blasting the Czar! Ironic and amusing both.

And guess what? It gets better. Ralphie owns a lot of stock. He apparently likes technology stocks, especially Cisco Systems of which he has $1.2 million worth (*Globe* says $1.6 million). Interesting in and of itself—but there's more to the story. Here we have a premier anti-capitalist owning over $1 million of a stock whose primary function is helping the Fortune 500 companies (you know, the cream of American capitalism!) work better and more efficiently! In short, to be all they can be.

In other words, all those horrible capitalists buy Cisco products so they can run more efficiently and exploit more people all over the world at a higher rate of return (don't forget, in Ralphie's worldview "corporate interests are the extremists") and Ralphie owns a piece of them.

Ralphie thus helps to support the increased and more efficient exploitation of the global masses while preaching against it. Ralphie's holdings allow him to get richer and richer the more the international capitalists exploit the masses more effectively. In short, Nader has a pretty big stake in what he calls "the forces of injustice" even as he rails against them.

I call that sweet—and quite a contradiction. And more than a tad hypocritical, wouldn't you say? Of course, lots of the liberal press seems willing to overlook such minor details and the background—or now hopefully foreground—of this saintly public figure.

Take Molly Ivins. You know Molly, she's the columnist who is always all over rich Republicans, especially George Bush and George W. Bush. As late as July 16 she was steadfastly maintaining that Nader *"lives on $25,000 a year and puts the rest into the public interest groups that he's set up around the country.* He's done more real good for this country than both the other candidates added together and multiplied." You betcha! Hasn't done too bad for himself either.

In fact, it turns out Nader made $512,000 in the last sixteen months. Not bad for a guy who looks like he really could use a new suit and some new shoes. Not bad for a guy pleading poverty at every turn. Not bad for such a wonderful humanitarian. In fact, it's not bad for a greedy capitalist.

Now all of this would simply be inside baseball on some dour public figure with a huge bank account, spouting a lot of warmed-over socialist rhetoric except for the fact that in the presidential election of 2000, the Greens could actually do some good and important work. This election cycle, Ralphie could turn out to be what Lenin once affectionately and tastefully termed a "poleznyi duraki" or "useful idiot," someone who serves the interests of your party and its objectives without meaning to.

Assuming Ralphie actually gets out and campaigns a little and especially if he can hoodwink the League of Women Voters into staging a "debate" with him and Buchanan, he can have a very worthwhile impact on November's election outcome. In fact, if George W. thinks about it, he should push for debates with both Nader and Buchanan as well as Gore.

As things now stand though, I'm just a little concerned about Nader's current campaign strategy to target non-voters. When he declared in a recent press conference I watched, "We must reach the non-voter," I got concerned. That's a truly bad idea on which to launch a political effort! It won't work. Apparently Ralphie and his advisors are banking a lot on Pearl Jam having registration cards at their performances but I doubt there will be much follow up from that source!

The last person I know who tried targeting non-voters in Maine was Bob Monks and I can tell you it did not work. People don't vote because they are against "the duopoly." In my experience, people don't vote because they are lazy, uninterested, and don't really care about the political system or who runs it. Or they are quite happy with the way things are going and they don't see a threat to their interests no matter who wins.

But assume the Green crusade actually reaches out to voters as opposed to non-voters (which I hope it will), it could have quite an impact. Led by Nader, the Greens *could* actually help elect George W.! In fact, if Nader breaks 10 percent on Election Day, they *will* elect George W.

Now I personally think George W. should win it on his merits. For me, the choice is quite clear and there *is* a real choice in this election despite all Nader's talk of a "duopoly." Bush wants to cut the present tax rates. Gore does not. Bush wants new wage earners to have a choice as to whether or not a small portion of their social security withholding taxes go into a private retirement fund which could invest in the stock market (so they can own Cisco Systems too!). Gore does not. Bush doesn't want to ban "soft money" in campaigns, Gore does. Bush wants a national and theatre missile defense system as soon as possible whether the Russians like it or not. Gore is far more hesitant and accommodating to Russia's (and others') wishes. And so on.

But back to Ralphie. Ralphie could turn out to be a nice little insurance policy for W. The Greens normally take 65–75 percent of their vote from the Democrats and Independents and in this case, the capitalist-bashing Ralphie may even take some votes away from Buchanan and the Reform Party. In fact, I bet Ralphie finishes higher than Buchanan.

I think Nader and the Greens could be a factor in a lot of states such as California, Michigan, Ohio, Colorado, Oregon, Washington, Wisconsin, and Maine. In this case—and this election—for the Republicans at least, Ralphie could well turn out to be one of Lenin's useful idiots.

So I guess there's a lot to like about Ralphie and his run:

Delicious irony.

Smoking out his huge personal fortune.

Electing the right president.

I say: "Run Ralphie, Run."

POSTSCRIPT

Written in August of 2000, this essay generated a great deal of controversy and personal attacks on me; strangely enough, mostly from Democrats. In the end, Ralph served well in fulfilling my prophecy, getting votes over 2 percent or 97,000 votes in Florida alone.

The majority of those votes came from Al Gore.

Arrogance: A Fable

$\mathscr{O}$nce upon a time in the Great Northern Forest of a parallel universe far, far away, there was a cute but annoying little hedgehog who insisted on building a boat for all the creatures of the forest whether they wanted one or not. Some of the forest creatures said he would lead them to the Promised Land, but others said he wanted to build the boat just so he could be its captain.

But none of this mattered because the hedgehog had the time and the money and the inclination to build a boat every year if he wished. So he went ahead and built the boat, never consulting any of the beavers or woodpeckers or any other creatures who worked with wood for a living. "What do they know?" he said. "Besides, I'm too pretty."

It was, if the truth be told, a strange craft. The bow was wider than the stern and there were a number of weird appendages dragging in the water, the motor was located on the side, and one of the sails was up-side down. From the beginning it looked quite odd. It even called for a crew of nine, none of whom had ever owned any boats. "But that way they won't be biased," he said.

Three owls who watched the boat being launched shook their heads. "If he'd taken my boat building class, I'd have flunked him," said one. "I don't think he's taken anybody's class," said the other. "I think he's in a class by himself," said the third.

Soon the boat was launched with considerable fanfare and lots of forest creatures were lured on board even though there were many questions about just how river-worthy it was. A magnificent legal eagle said,

131

"That boat won't be able to get to 'bank' once it gets going," and the chief forest ranger said, "This is a very bad idea; I watched it being built and it will be a disaster."

"Dupes, dupes," cried the hedgehog and his followers. This set in motion a highly amusing scenario in which anybody who had any questions about the boat, the captain, the crew, or the destination were all called "dupes" no matter who they were or how much they knew about boat building.

Well, as soon as the boat started down the river, there were problems. It began to leak and careened wildly from rock to rock. Soon many of the passengers were "sprawled" all over the decks. Some of the smarter and quicker forest animals began to abandon ship crying, "This isn't going to make it. I knew something was wrong when the crew kept looking back off the stern instead of the bow, but they said that was the way things were going to be done from now on."

But the hedgehog stayed at the wheel, having the time of his life yelling, "I'm on the bridge. I'm in command." He especially liked it when some of his young supporters, not yet in long pants, kept chirping, "It's a wonderful craft, it's a wonderful craft, they're all jealous. His first mate got very emotional and cried at the drop of a hat, tears running down her cheeks, "I love the forest. I love the forest."

But at just the moment the boat was definitely sinking, out of the woods came a whole troop of steely-eyed, gerbil-looking creatures who were chattering like a bunch of monkeys.

"It's the stern gerbils, it's the stern gerbils," cried the forest people. The stern gerbils were well known in the forest for always telling everybody else what to do and acting high and mighty and giving directions and being cross with anybody who asked them, "Are you sure you're right?" They were quite a nuisance to just about everybody in the forest although they had a very high opinion of themselves. They would get quite mad if anyone criticized them or ever pointed out that some of their statements were wrong.

"My god," said one of the owls, "the stern gerbils are swimming toward the sinking ship. You seldom see that."

Not only did the gerbils swim toward the ship, they quickly clamored aboard. Chattering loudly, they ran madly around the ship bumping into the hedgehog's crew and shouting, "Do this. Do that. Stop the engine. Pull up the sail. Turn around." The head gerbil even raced up onto the bridge and tried to grab the wheel from the hedgehog. "Let me try. Let me try," he said.

But the hedgehog wouldn't let go of the wheel of his ship although while they were struggling, the boat started to turn sideways. "Dupes. Dupes," the hedgehog kept yelling at the onlookers as the boat lurched down the stream. The crew tried to keep the stern gerbils from getting control of the pumps and the sails and the motor but it was hard because the gerbils were running everywhere as if the boat was theirs.

Then, undeterred at not being able to take the wheel, the head stern gerbil began bellowing toward the shore, "Sure it's broken. Sure it's sinking. We all know that. The hedgehog should have consulted with us before he built the thing. But don't worry, come back on board and once we get around the next bend, out of sight, we'll fix it."

Hearing that, the forest creatures began to shake their heads. "Say what?" said one, "Does he think we just fell off the mushroom truck? It sounds like a risky scheme to me. Although the stern gerbils make a lot of noise, they often get things wrong—remember the highway they didn't want built and that fine heating plant they want to shut down for no good reason."

"That head stern gerbil is a hoot," said one of the owls.

And, lo and behold, the forest creatures seemed to have a point because the boat took on more and more water. All the while the hedgehog kept shaking his fist at the shore, yelling, "Dupes, dupes," and some of the gerbils were shouting, "It's broken but we can still fix it."

Another of the stern gerbils cried, "It's not over. The governor of the forest will fix it, he'll appoint a new crew and they'll fix it just the way we want."

"I wouldn't hold my breath for that; I think the stern gerbils have worn out their welcome with the governor," said one of the owls, winking at his friends.

The boat finally sank under the swirling current. Things had turned out looking pretty well for the dupes and pretty bad for the stern gerbils and the hedgehog.

Still, one of the smarter, if more cynical, stern gerbils said as he swam to shore, "Who cares, we'll raise a lot of money off this fiasco and sign up some new gerbils."

By nightfall, all was quiet once again in the forest.

The hedgehog was already at work on his new boat, "an herbal submarine." But before he really got going, he went to his library and ripped the covers off all his nature field guides and pasted on new ones. Then he stood over his coffee table and admired his handiwork: *The Dupe Society Field Guide to North American Birds*, *The Dupe Society Field Guide to Mushrooms*, and *The Dupe Society Field Guide to the Northern Forest*.

"I'll teach them to oppose me," he said. "Maybe next year if I have more time, I'll write my own guides. I know a lot more than they do about everything in the forest."

For their part, the head stern gerbil and his troop went back to their cave (which was appropriately named "The Cave of Absolute Doom and Gloom") and into the special "Parts Per Billion" room where all their key decisions were made. He and his followers sat around and tried to think of how to keep their names in the forest papers so the other animals wouldn't forget who they were.

"We've lost four in a row," said one of the newer gerbils, "maybe we should rethink our goals." "Or our methods," added another. "Or our attitude," chimed in yet another, "The other creatures of the forest didn't look all that sad when we got pitched into the water." "Yeah, a lot of them were even clapping."

But before that discussion could get up much of a head of steam, the head stern gerbil and his "council" had all three dissidents banished to the gerbil's reeducation camp at the Kampuchea miniature golf course on the edge of the forest. This was the same miniature golf course where, it was believed, the stern gerbils got most of their information about the real forest.

Part V

ISSUES IN DEMOCRACY

Candidate Positioning

$\mathcal{W}$hile voters are often fond of saying they decide their electoral choice based on something called "the issues," in fact, many decide on other factors such as party affiliation, personality, and image.

Yet issues remain both a challenge and an opportunity for candidates. In Maine, the most important positioning for a candidate is in the middle of the political spectrum. This means being judged "not too far right" and "not too far left." A large plurality of Maine voters self-identify themselves as "moderate," followed by "conservative," and then "liberal."

Most successful candidates in Maine's recent political history have come from the middle or moderate portion of the political spectrum. Usually in Republican primaries, the less conservative candidate wins and usually in Democratic primaries, the less liberal candidate wins.

But candidates do not have free reign in positioning themselves for the general election. Usually, they are pushed to the right or to the left by the dynamics of their primary situation and by the public's perceptions of their position.

In the gubernatorial race for 2002, the situation of Congressman John Baldacci is illustrative. A popular four-term, Democratic incumbent, Baldacci is a likeable, hard-working office holder, anxious to please and help. His current approval rating is in the low 70 percent so he starts off the race for the Blaine House with a good base, some experience, and a real desire and hunger to leave the Washington scene and move back to Maine. In fact, he has commuted to Washington for six years, keeping his family back here.

Although he had a tough primary battle in 1994, his first time out, winning a narrow 27 percent to 23 percent victory over Jim Mitchell and five other candidates, he then defeated his Republican opponent, Rick Bennett, by a margin of 46 percent to 41 percent while the Independent, John Michael got 8.8 percent of the vote and Charles Fitzgerald the Green got 4.7 percent.

From then on, Baldacci only drew weak and underfunded opponents, winning 73 percent to 23 percent over Paul Young in 1996, 76 percent to 24 percent over Jonathan Reisman in 1998, and 72 percent over Dick Campbell in 2000.

These victories added to Baldacci's mantel of invincibility and when he indicated in 2000 that he wished to run for the governorship in 2002, many Democratic Party faithful rallied around him and many Republicans were quick to concede both his front-runner status and the seriousness of his chances. Yet I saw a number of obstacles to his becoming governor. These included not being tested in a close race for eight years, residual opposition within the Democratic Party centered in the old Brennan wing, his need to provide a vision for his proposed governorship, and a potential problem in issue positioning.

It is here he faces "Baldacci's conundrums."

His first conundrum is that his high surface numbers are based primarily on name recognition for both his style and his substance have yet to be proven in the 1st Congressional District. In other words, over 70 percent of the people of Maine say he has done a good job as Congressman but many do not know what kind of governor he would make, and Maine people have traditionally wanted different things in their governors and senators than their congresspeople.

His second conundrum is what to do about Joe Brennan. Brennan, who understands exit polling as well as anybody in the game, knows that on Election Day of 1996, he was actually ahead in the Senate race until the 4 to 6 PM surge in the 2nd District for Susan Collins kicked in. In fact, Maine Public Broadcasting projected Brennan the winner based on the day's early returns from southern Maine.

But in the heart of Baldacci country (from Bangor north), Brennan ended up running far below Baldacci's numbers and just below the necessary Democratic levels for victory. Brennan and others seem to blame Baldacci for a lack of support on his home turf. In any case, there appear to be few hard core Brennanistas who believe Baldacci did all he could to help ensure Joe's victory in such a close race.

On balance then, Brennan would seem to have little reason to be enthusiastic about Baldacci in the Blaine House and who among long time and close Brennan supporters can blame him? Brennan may in fact go outside the party and choose to support his long time friend and associate, David Flanagan, the former head of Central Maine Power. With his newly found wealth from the sale of the company, Flannagan could finance his own campaign.

It is not just Republicans and old Brennanistas who oppose the Baldacci coronation. The more liberal wing of the Democratic Party, especially in the 1st Congressional District, may well have found a strong opponent for Baldacci in the Democratic primary, Chellie Pingree.

There is also the conundrum of Baldacci's issue shifts. Recently, he has moved rather precipitously toward gun control, telling a stunned national reporter that he supports "tighter gun control" and Clinton's Eight Points for gun control.

Again, this may seem to some like a clever move to engender political support in Maine's somewhat more liberal 1st District, but it may turn out to be too clever by half if and when the rest of the state finds out about it.

Baldacci was elected with the extensive support of the Sportsman's Alliance of Maine and while "gun control" in the abstract is somewhat popular among urban and suburban Democrats in southern Maine, it is not with rural or northern ones. This recent shift probably will not hurt him much in his reelection bid for Congress, given the likely weakness of his Republican challengers, but it will most likely come back to haunt him in a serious way in his race for governor.

Gun control remains a wedge issue in northern, western, and eastern Maine and the men and women of Maine who hunt and fish have traditionally put into office our governors. They may not be allowed to forget Baldacci's about-face on this vital issue to them.

Finally, there is the conundrum of business support. Baldacci cannot win the general election without major funding support from Maine's business community and he has worked long and hard to project a carefully crafted image of concern for business in Maine.

Baldacci continues to court Maine business leaders with vigor and skill, projecting both an image of inevitability and a personally engaging style of "I will listen to you."

Now, no one should ever underestimate the collective capacity of the Maine business community to be gulled. One has only to think of their previous shutting down of the highly effective "United for Maine" effort or their subsequent donations to the political action committees of both Speaker John Martin and Senate President Charley Pray to question both their will and their sanity on some substantive political matters, but the present situation is actually far more serious and menacing.

The worker's compensation reforms currently operative in Maine are the most important sea change in Maine's business climate in the last thirty years. They represent the absolutely vital element in keeping Maine's economy moving forward. They are why Maine's business climate is positive rather than negative as we approach 2000 and they have fueled job creation in Maine ever since they were enacted.

I also believe these reforms were one very important reason why Angus King ran for a second term, fearing they would be overturned in a heartbeat by the next governor were he or she to be a Democrat who danced to organized labor's tune.

And so they may well be.

Baldacci has thus far skillfully danced around the issue, citing his small business background and talking vaguely about "access" and "listening to both sides." But should he have to face the business community head on with specific and written promises to the business community—if they are smart enough to ask for them—he may fall between two stools. By making such pledges, he would open himself up to criticism from the center and left wings of the Democratic Party and make trouble for himself especially among the union faithful in the 1st District. Hence the conundrum.

A most interesting question now surfaces.

Do prominent business leaders such as Peter Vigue of Cianbro, Alan Cameron of BIW, and others seriously believe that in 2003, when the fat hits the fire over gutting the worker's compensation reforms, that Governor Baldacci will return their calls—let alone put their arguments ahead of those from the AFL/CIO or Severin Beliveau or Pat McTeague—when crunch time comes?

Congressman John Baldacci hopes they do.

His positioning on the issues, far enough left to win the primary but not so far as to hurt himself in the general election must be balanced by the realities of the 2002 gubernatorial race. With Maine's so called "Clean Election" guidelines in place, Baldacci will not only face a Republican challenge and an Independent one in the form of David Flanagan, he will also face a determined challenge from the left in the general election.

Jonathan Carter will have $1.2 million with which to mount a campaign which is extremely likely to eat away at Baldacci's left portion of his coalition in the fall. The only place to replace those lost liberal votes is in the political center and Baldacci will have to be most skillful to move left, then right, and not get caught on more than one bull's-eye.

In this race, skillful issue positioning and fluid movement will be the key to success and I would bestow on Baldacci the title "Lovely Mover" if he can pull it off.

In the Abortion Universe

Is Maine a pro-Choice state or a pro-Life state?

Normally, this is a question only asked by the truly committed or by the nervous first time politician seeking to make a name for herself or himself. In fact, the question is usually asked in a way that yields very little in the way of operational significance.

The following essay, written during the summer of 1999, reflects on the enduring realities of the abortion situation in Maine. Although opponents of the so-called partial birth abortion procedure began with a big lead but ended up losing by a margin of 58 percent to 42 percent. As indicated below, the swing vote was males who didn't care much about abortion. Exit polling indicated that they had turned against the ban by a ratio of 60–40 percent, thus providing the No side with its margin of victory.

Let's look at the abortion universe with a clinical eye. Let's look at it in a way which yields the most operational significance in terms of Maine politics.

First, if you examine the positions of the major state office holders, Maine looks very much like a pro-Choice state. Governor King, Senators Snowe and Collins, as well as Representatives Allen and Baldacci all support a woman's right to choose. No matter what their personal beliefs about abortion, they support something which looks to most like a pro-Choice position. And it's been that way for a long time. Senators Cohen and Hathaway as well as Governor McKernan were always pro-Choice, and Senators Muskie and Mitchell and Governor Brennan ended up pro-Choice as well.

143

Second, if you look at the Maine legislature, Maine looks very much like a pro-Choice state. The legislature hardly ever passes a pro-Life bill and pro-Choice lobbyists are able to make their voices heard on a variety of issues relating to choice. In fact, the bill before the voters this November was rejected twice already by the legislature.

Third, if you ask Maine people a basic positioning question such as are they "pro-Choice or pro-Life" at least six out of ten will say they are "pro-Choice" as defined in "a woman's body is her own" or "a woman should have the choice where it concerns her body."

Looking at the abortion issue below the surface, however, raises some very interesting questions about these assumptions especially in an off year, low turnout election. Unpacking voter self-arrangement in a different way can be very instructive.

If you ask Maine people to self-define themselves along an abortion spectrum and let them give you their position, for example, you get a most challenging profile. Usually at any given time in Maine, voters will arrange themselves along the abortion spectrum as follows:

12–15 percent of Maine people oppose all abortions.

10 percent of Maine people oppose all abortions except those to save the life of the mother.

35–40 percent of Maine people support all abortions if a woman needs or wants one.

15 percent of Maine people don't know where they stand on abortion and don't really want to stand anywhere.

The key to defining Maine in terms of its position on the abortion spectrum thus rests with the remaining 25 percent-plus of Maine people who oppose abortions except to (1) save the life of the mother and (2) in cases of rape or (3) incest. This is the most important cohort for political purposes.

How you count this group is very important. Is this cohort "pro-Choice," because those in it are for abortions, or is it "pro-Life" because those in it oppose other types of abortions?

If you count this group as pro-Choice, Maine is solidly a pro-Choice state. If you count this group as pro-Life, Maine is a marginally pro-Life state. So right away, in the real world of electoral politics, you need to know what is the operational significance of your positioning of that group in any given election and which portion of that cohort can be moved by campaign messages.

Should you target them as pro-Life or pro-Choice?

Both sides have to take them into account in the upcoming referendum for this November; voters in Maine have, for the first time in decades, a chance to vote on an abortion issue. There is an item on the ballot that would ban "a specific abortion procedure to be defined in law except in cases where the life of the mother is in danger." The very question seems tailored for ambiguity and thus very lively political ballot measure campaigns.

Both sides will deal with that ambiguity by pushing the choice to the farthest poles of good versus evil as they can, bringing the rest of us along for the ride if they can.

If you are pro-Life, therefore, you call this procedure a "Partial Birth Abortion." If you are pro-Choice, you call it a "Late Term Abortion."

If this seems pretty obscure and irrelevant to you, rest assured it is very important to many of the 88,000 Maine people who signed petitions to get this on the ballot and to the tens of thousands of Maine people who will oppose it just as vigorously.

The procedure in question proposed for banning does sound pretty gruesome although Dr. Dora Ann Mills, Director of the Maine Health Service, insists that third-term trimester abortion procedures have only been used twice in the last sixteen years here in Maine.

Interestingly enough, most people in Maine already know where they stand on abortion. In fact, the numbers I cited above have changed hardly at all over the last twenty years!

Those who are for abortion aren't going to change their minds in the next four months and those who are against abortion aren't about to change their minds either.

When the 1999 campaign is over, those who oppose abortion now will still oppose it and those who support it now will still support it.

Obviously, given the overall balance in the state, however, some people will have to change their minds—or least get tuned into the debate and turned out to vote in order for one side or the other to win conclusively.

Who then will be the most important group in November in determining the fate of *this specific abortion proposal?*

Who will be the swing vote on this issue?

Who will have to be the target audience for both sides?

Who will have to be made to see the "rightness" of either position?
Who will turn the tide in November?

The answer is "males."

And not just any males.

This election will be decided by males who don't care about the issue.

November's outcome will *not* be decided by the women or the men already firmly in the pro-Life or pro-Choice camp, those already committed to their particular stand on abortion.

This election will be decided by males who at this point have no interest in the procedure, no interest in the debate, and no interest in the outcome of the referendum.

To understand this, you need to appreciate that while men arrange themselves across the abortion spectrum in much the same way women do—in polling terms, we say their *distribution* is roughly comparable—they do not care as deeply as women about this issue. To examine the true impact of an issue on a demographic or psychographic group, to understand it as a voting trigger, you have to move beyond distribution to the *intensity* of that distribution. How strongly is that view held by the group in question?

In terms of the law of large numbers, relatively few males, especially in any of the swing categories, put abortion as a top issue for themselves. Thus in polling terms, the abortion issue lacks *intensity* for them. Left to their own devices, they simply don't and won't care much about it and unless stimulated, probably wouldn't vote on it.

Obviously, opponents and proponents will have no problem getting out their core voters, including their male supporters. The challenge to both sides will be to get the other males—the males who do not like this issue and who do not care very much about it—to care on Election Day and vote one way or the other.

Thus, when we look back next December on this fall's struggle over "Partial Birth/Late Term" abortion, we are likely to see that over $1,000,000 will have been spent contesting a procedure which has been used twice in the last sixteen years and that the principle decision makers in this struggle will have been males who don't care about the issue!

Who says issues in a democracy can't be intriguing and fun?

The Right to Arm Bears?

$\mathcal{A}$uthor Karen Blixen once wrote, "True hunters are in love with the animals they hunt, but that love is not reciprocated." As a lifelong hunter and fisherman and a registered Maine Guide for over twenty years, I have always been moved by the inherent poignancy of that statement and its implications. It also helps to explain some of our internal paradoxes such as wanting to protect deer from coyotes and wolves so there will be more of them for us to kill every fall.

Recently, I saw a bumper sticker in Portland that read "Support your right to arm bears." That slogan is, I think, an important way to conceptualize the way people who don't hunt and those who do have intertwined the related but not identical issues of gun ownership and hunting.

The contemporary issues of gun ownership will be featured and explored more fully in a future column. But for now, true hunters would have to admit that arming bears would make the contest between man and animal fairer and certainly more challenging. They also might be more in favor of gun control measures for bears, including thirty-day waiting periods, paw printing, and background checks on the most violent of bruins. In some locales, they might even oppose handgun ownership for bears.

Often, organizations such as the National Rifle Association (NRA) make it very difficult for hunters by insisting on pushing to the outer limits gun ownership claims. The interests of hunters and the NRA are not always identical. Hunters, for example, do not need assault rifles for woods work. Nor do they need armor piercing bullets. Sometimes, the very intransigence of the NRA puts it in the same illogical camp as the most rapid anti-hunter, anti-gun owner groups and the ensuing cross-fire hurts hunters more than they realize.

Here in Maine, we are fortunate to have an organization which, while defending gun owners on important issues, focuses much more fully on the aspects which truly matter most to those of us who hunt and fish in Maine.

Interestingly enough, while hunting and fishing license holders have actually declined somewhat over the last ten years here in Maine, The Sportsman's Alliance of Maine (SAM) has grown significantly.

SAM now has 14,000 members. Fourteen thousand members is more than the Maine Audubon Society and the Natural Resources of Maine combined. Think of the policy implications of that for a moment! Also, equally important, SAM serves as the most important symbolic referent for the 250,000 men and women who hunt and fish in Maine. It is the most important authority spokesperson for the interests of Maine hunter and fishermen and women.

When SAM speaks, sportsmen and women listen.

Under the very able direction of George Smith, SAM has seen its annual budget rise tenfold from $50,000 to over $500,000 a year and it has become a powerful political force both within the legislature and in terms of ballot measure issues. Astute and savvy, Smith knows the issues of the out-of-doors as well as anyone in the state. Because he is a hard core hunter and fisherman and his right-wing, conservative Republican credentials are impeccable, when he takes a position, many pay attention across the political spectrum and even opponents are respectful. Along with Harry Vanderweide, Paul Jacques, Ken Allen, Roberta Scruggs, and Tom Hennessey, George Smith is one of the few authentic voices speaking for the Maine hunting and fishing scenes.

That is why it is so important that SAM has come out so strongly in favor of Question 7, the $50 million public access bond this November.

In fact, for those who hunt and fish, snowmobile, trap, and snowshoe, or just enjoy a walk in the woods, *Question 7 is the most important issue on the ballot, not just for this year, but for this decade.*

We need to hear the voice of Maine's sportsmen and women and we need to hear it loud and clear.

Sportsmen and women know how important access is. The finest trout stream or lake is not of much value to sportsmen and women if they can't have access to it. The most beautiful snowmobile in the world is just a lawn ornament if there are insufficient trails.

Wildlife habitat needs to be protected and deer yards purchased so they can continue to perform their life-sustaining functions. Islands along the Maine coast and precious lake and river frontage are in danger of development. Streams and mountains have to be put off-limits for development or destruction while keeping access for those who hunt and fish.

Every year, thousands and thousands of acres of Maine land go off-limits to hunters and fishermen through development, posting, and changed forest practices. Every year, Maine snowmobilers and hikers and hunters see more and more access denied. Sprawl is a real and growing problem. Those who love the out of doors are losing access at an alarming rate statewide. Everyone who spends a lot of time in the out of doors has seen a favorite place placed off-limits, developed out of existence.

Make no mistake about what is the issue this fall with Question 7. It is all about access. Not just for us but for our children and our grandchildren. Question 7 gives us one last chance to save our priceless Maine heritage; to enable us to pass it on to our children and our grandchildren.

Access is the key. Access to the streams and lakes and mountains, the islands and fields, the priceless natural opportunities which are such a vital part of the Maine heritage, so integral to our very special "Wild, Wild East."

In the coming debate, do not be misled by the wild posturing of those who don't care that future generations will be denied the true Maine experience.

Don't be misled by those misguided individuals bent on self-promotion at the expense of those of us who love and use the out-of-doors and want to pass that priceless Maine heritage on to our children and our grandchildren.

Beware of those using the Access Referendum to further their political agendas on other issues. This referendum is not about forest policy, or about a National Park, or the right to bear arms or even about the right to arm bears.

Don't be misled by those ideologues trapped in some weird time warp from the 1950s who do not realize that if we don't make more land public and protect our access to it, somebody else will make it private and shut off that access.

Don't be misled by those who would try to set Mainer against Mainer by making an artificial distinction between the needs of northern and southern Maine.

Access is not just a northern problem. Access is not just a southern problem. Access is not just a coastal problem. Access is not just an inland problem.

Access is a problem for all of us.

Our priceless Maine heritage of today and tomorrow should not be made a political football for those who neither understand nor care about the true future of the out-of-doors here in Maine.

In the coming weeks, be guided by those who know and love the out-of-doors—not by those driven by self-promotion.

Be guided by those who have no political ax to grind, who know and love the wilderness experience and want to protect it for future generations.

Be guided by what you personally want to preserve of Maine's priceless outdoor heritage, a heritage which is slipping away bit by bit, year by year.

In the coming debate, listen to such hard core outdoor groups as SAM, the Maine Snowmobile Association, the Maine Campground Owners Association, the Maine Trappers Association, The Maine Bowhunters Association, Ducks Unlimited, Maine Council of Trout Unlimited, and the Ruffed Grouse Society.

They all know the "real" Maine and all are urging their members to support Question 7, the Access Bond Issue. All understand what is at stake.

This is a magnificent group of organizations who know the real Maine, up close and personal. They know how important passage of this bond is for all of us.

They know—as we all should—that if we don't make more Maine land public, somebody—and soon—will make it private and those who love the out-of-doors and treasure enjoying "The Wild, Wild East" will be denied more and more access.

Access is the key. Question 7 provides the access to our priceless Maine heritage, not just for us but for those generations of Maine people yet to come.

If Question 7 doesn't pass, we all lose. Bears and trout, deer and moose, men and women, Maine people of all ages. Generations yet to come.

We all lose.

POSTSCRIPT

Question 7 passed by a margin of 63 percent to 47 percent, carrying all counties in Maine, showing that Maine people continue to support the idea of preserving special places for generations to come and that the sentiment in this regard is statewide, not just regional.

Not on the Ballot

For me, October is always such an exciting month. October means getting ready for elections and elections mean opportunities for people to get out and support their candidates and their causes, to leave their stamp on important issues of the day. In a democracy, it is imperative that citizens recognize their power to shape their own destinies by placing as much symbolic value as they can on the issues that appeal to them.

Thus far, however, there has never been a referendum in Maine on the question of Indian gambling. For my part, I hope this changes. I really want Maine's Passamaquoddies to have a casino up in Washington County. I see a casino up there on Native American land as a win, win, win situation.

I come to the issue honestly enough.

When we left Hartford in 1950 and moved to Niantic, Connecticut, my father became fast friends with a Nehantic Indian named Lievy Huntley (what a great name for a Native American!). Lievy was reputed to be the last of the Nehantics and he more than lived up to his name. He hunted year round and would bring deer to our house in every season to have my father cut it up on his band saw.

As a kid, I had always idolized Crazy Horse and despised Custer, thinking him a vainglorious bumbler. And I always became an Indian when we kids played Cowboys and Indians so I was very, very impressed with having a real Indian for a friend. Lievy was a wonderful, kind, and generous man and never seemed to mind a kid tagging along on his various expeditions.

Every October, the Niantic Bay opened for scalloping and if you had a permit you could go opening day and even stay out of school to go scalloping. Rather like getting out of school to pick potatoes up in Aroostook County, but a lot more fun I'll bet.

So I not only got to go scalloping early in the morning with Lievy, but after we'd gotten our five bushels and sold them, I went to school, late, swaggering in dripping big black boots, with a seagull feather in my hair and $5 in my pocket and when the teacher asked where I'd been, I could honestly say, "I'd been scalloping with my Indian friend." In 1950 in the Niantic Center School, that was about as cool as you could get.

Actually, I thought we were going to be even cooler the night I went down into our cellar to find my father and Lievy hunched over behind the furnace and making strange noises and signs. This went on for a long time. When I crept back upstairs, I was sure we were being initiated into the tribe (of course, who knows what we would think today of two grown men hiding down behind the furnace). What a disappointment to learn Lievy was just some high potentate in the local Masons and was teaching my father how to become a Mason. A Mason, for god's sake! Not a Nehantic, or a Pequot, or a Mohegan—a Mason.

Once I thought my sister and I were going to make it into the tribe on our own. It was a cold but sunny January day and we looked out our window to see a deer swimming across the ocean from an island. It must have swum two miles before it tottered up onto the rocks in front of our house. Exhausted, it stood there shaking while we got a rope and I lassoed it. Quite a thrill, that, being dragged over the icy rocks by a deer. But we hung on for dear life and my sister and I managed to pull it down and tie its hooves together just like a calf.

We were pretty excited and when I thought how impressed Lievy would be when we brought him a live deer, I was sure we were going to get into his tribe on this accomplishment alone. Unfortunately for us, but fortunately for the deer, my mother came out of the house and insisted we cart the deer in my father's truck over to Rocky Neck State Park and let it go. What a bummer! I think my mother was in the Old Lyme Garden Club as well as the Audubon Society.

Lievy got a big kick out of the story and probably tracked down the deer afterwards because we told him exactly where we'd released it and it was undoubtedly too tired to move far. Lievy was a pretty cheerful guy, except when he got going on about land and how it was all taken away from the Indians. We would be in the middle of the Niantic Bay and he would point to the shore, now dotted with houses and gas stations and bait stores and say, "Once that all belonged to us." And I suppose it had.

I never forgot his sadness about land and I was very happy to learn about the later rise of the Mohegans and the Pequots through gambling. I visited Foxwoods Casino in Ledyard, Connecticut last spring and was bowled over by the entire complex. It rises up like some New World Taj Mahal in the middle of the woods in northeastern Connecticut.

The whole thing is very, very impressive.

First, there is now the largest casino in the world at Foxwoods (owned by the Mashantucket Pequots) with another one close by in Uncasville (owned by the Mohegans). Over 1.2 million people spend over $1 billion a year.

Second, there is a $190 million museum run by and for and of Native Americans with all you ever wanted to know about the eastern Indians and then some, including history going back to the last Ice Age. Third, the casinos throw off hundreds of millions of dollars to the state in lieu of taxes. Just think what Maine could do with an extra $200 million a year in state revenues!

Fourth, Indians run the fire department and the police department and the museum and the pride you feel emanating from them is palpable. Fifth, the Indians now have so much money they are now buying back land around the casinos so they are regaining that portion of their heritage.

Sixth, and this is probably the best part, the tribes own hydrofoils to bring over all the gamblers from Long Island and truck them from port to casino on trains, giving them free rides home if they lose all their money. So, relieved of the burden of how to get home, some of them do leave it all behind for the Indians to turn into more land. Are you kidding me? This is fantastic.

So I thought it would be something of a slam dunk to duplicate Foxwoods in Washington County on Passamaquoddy land. Of course, it would have to be on a smaller scale since there are fewer Canadians and they have less money than people in Connecticut, Rhode Island, and New York. But what a great idea for the whole state, I thought.

Such a project would reduce unemployment in Washington County, get much needed revenues to the state, increase the legitimate and long-denied power of the Indians, and generally make for economic development in a part of Maine currently known primarily for its scenery, its blueberries, and its very hard way of life.

Not so, said the governor. He's against gambling of all types. Not so, said the Maine Legislature ("We'd have to have gambling at Old Orchard Beach too"). Not so, said the Indian representative I spoke with who seemed supremely uninterested in the plan. Of course white people have been coming along with rotten ideas for Indians for over three hundred years so that might have something to do with it. And I probably sounded a little hyper talking up the idea.

But I'm pretty sure I could win a statewide referendum on the issue. And boy, would I like to try. I think it would make Lievy happy wherever he is in the Happy Hunting Grounds in the sky.

Gay Rights III

$\mathscr{I}$n recent years, Maine people have looked at the question of Gay Rights in three separate elections. In the first, proponents of Gay Rights won, in the second (a special election) they lost. The third, held during the presidential election of 2000, also saw proponents of Gay Rights losing. Yet during this entire period, the overall opinion of Mainers concerning Gay Rights did not change. In fact, the polling remained remarkably consistent. What varied from 1996 through 2000, was the quality of the campaigns waged for and against Gay Rights. This chapter, written during the third campaign, captures the dimensions of that issue and its demographic and psychographic aspects.

"I am gay."

These three simple words, acknowledging the reality of one's sexual orientation, an orientation provided by inherited genetic material, are freighted with heavy and powerful meaning.

Were I to utter them today, would my social, political, and economic life here in Maine be different than it was before?

As we enter the third referendum in a half dozen years on this subject, the expectations each of us has as to the true import of those three words become of paramount importance.

The question "Would things be different?" lies at the heart of the debate and for many, represents the critical point of departure on this issue. When supporters of Gay Rights won the first referendum, they did so because they convinced a majority of Mainers that gay men and lesbians should have *the same rights* as the rest of the population.

When opponents of Gay Rights won the second referendum, they did so because they convinced a majority of those who voted in that special election that gay men and lesbians should not have *special rights.*

But beyond this simple framing of the two debates there was—and there remains—a difficult perceptional problem for those of us who support gay rights. There is currently a seemingly unbridgeable gulf in practical political terms which supporters of gay rights must bridge if they are to win in November. I believe that gulf comes from one powerful set of perceptions reflecting the need for additional laws to protect gay men and lesbians from discrimination in the workplace, in living situations, and in general.

Today, a majority of Maine people—rightly or wrongly—do not believe that there is discrimination against gay men and lesbians in Maine. Most who live in Maine, especially in the small towns of Maine, do not believe that there is discrimination in their town or their state. There may be discrimination in other places in the United State, but there is no discernable discrimination in the Maine that they know. So they do not believe that a remedy is needed.

Now many—even a majority—of gay men and lesbians who live in Maine have a different point of view. Most would say that there is discrimination in Maine, in cities as well as in towns, in the country as well as in the suburbs, and there needs to be a legal remedy to make that discrimination less hurtful and less pervasive. They feel that there needs to be some legal protection for them as a class to undercut and eliminate such discrimination. They believe that saying "I am gay" puts them at some discernable level of risk.

Now I happen to believe that the gay men and lesbians are correct, that there is enough discrimination among enough people so that there is a need for this legislation. But that is very different from realizing that since most people in Maine do not believe there is discrimination, *you have to prove to them that there is as well as get them to vote for the proposed legislation.*

Supporters of gay rights have not proven their case to many in Maine that such discrimination exists. Without this validation, moderate voters may be unwilling to provide a remedy. They see no real problem and thus feel there is no need for a specific remedy.

Gay Rights I won because supporters were able to convince the electorate that gay rights were the same as other rights, that there was a continuum of discrimination which included other groups (Catholics, Francos, African Americans, etc.) as well as gays. In the final days of the campaign, supporters of gay rights were successful in appealing to the better instincts of Maine people by urging a no vote because "It's just not Maine" to discriminate.

In that context, "Maine" meant individual freedom and a philosophy of live and let live. It meant you did not have to believe in something specific you were dubious about; it simply meant you had to accept a higher (and easier to understand) concept.

For their part, opponents of gay rights won Gay Rights II because they were able to convince the electorate that gay rights were not linked to other rights but were in and of themselves, "special." And because supporters of gay rights abandoned their earlier, successful strategy of inclusion and took for granted the wildly inflated levels of support which appeared in a number of newspapers throughout the state, they ended up losing.

For it is true that some of those published polls indicated two-thirds of Maine people supported equal rights and this was taken to mean gay rights. That these polls were accepted at face value led supporters of gay rights to adopt an incorrect strategy.

In fact, supporters of gay rights made two fundamental errors: (1) when they took those polling artifacts at face value and (2) when they failed to enlist the support of others who had felt the lash of discrimination in earlier times (Catholics and Francos) and tried to win the referendum strictly on the rightness or wrongness of discrimination against gays and lesbians.

Thus the polling numbers themselves contributed to both of these assumptions and to the eventual defeat of those who supported gay rights. I believe that the various polling instruments were themselves at fault. Those polling efforts which were so wildly off the mark in projecting the outcome of the second referendum underscore the caveat that polling is 90 percent science and 10 percent art, but sometimes it is the "art" which is critical, especially in designing questionnaires for highly charged public policy issues.

When you are dealing with a highly charged issue and want to sample public opinion, you cannot simply ask the question a single way or take as gospel the results which do not give the respondent a real choice in answering the question.

For example, if you are adamantly opposed to gay rights but you know that the politically correct thing is to be for them and someone you don't know calls you up one evening to ask you your opinion, you are probably unlikely to blurt out all your prejudices in a five or ten minute phone call.

That is why to get a correct fix on the true levels of support for gay rights, you have to ask at least two questions: (1) Do you support equal rights for all, including gay men and women? and (2) Do you support special rights for gay men and women? The actual referendum numbers, the true reading of the political situation at any moment in time, will lie in between 1 and 2. Relying on just question 1 will inflate the support for gay rights beyond reality and relying on just question 2 will artificially cut that margin. But taken together, 1 and 2 can be combined to project the reality likely to obtain on Election Day.

What you need is an appreciation that the realities measured by (1) and (2) *when taken together*, give you a more accurate assessment of where the referendum on gay rights is at any particular time than any single question. Maine people did not—and do not—believe in special rights for anybody but a majority do believe in equal rights for all. In point of fact, there was little change in this aspect of the overall portrait of Maine voters in the two elections.

Beyond the perceptional differences, there is also the matter of religion. In addition to the "no need" argument, opponents of gay rights often take the Bible as a source of justification for opposing gay rights. Even when cloaked in smarmy rhetoric such as "God hates the sin but loves the sinner," the basic intolerance of this point of view irritates me no end. I see no reason at all to cede the religious high ground to those who term homosexuality a "sin."

I personally find it very difficult to believe that an all-knowing, loving God (such as is described in the New Testament) would create a whole class of genetically programmed sinners for whom there was no redemption save in denying their sexual orientation! For me, the categorical imperative of Jesus stating, "do unto others as you would have done to you" overrides all other imperatives from other parts of the Bible. I have no problem with the interrelated natures of religion, government, and society (and the clash of values that implies). I do have a problem with one segment of the religious community hijacking the cross for their personal agendas.

For me, the final argument for Gay Rights comes directly from the common sense answer to the statement with which we began. Say, "I am gay." Assume *you* were gay and born that way. Assume that in acknowledging who you are and will always be, you are now at the collective mercy of everybody in Maine. Would you honestly feel free to say these three words loudly and publicly and without fear?

If the answer is "yes," you should feel free to vote "No" in the upcoming Gay Rights referendum.

If the answer is "no," you should vote "Yes" in the upcoming referendum.

Maine is a better place for being more tolerant, not less.

Maine is a better place for being inclusive, not exclusive.

Maine is a better place for holding to the motto of "live and let live."

Discrimination?

Let's say, "It's just not Maine" one more time.

Part VI

PSYCHOGRAPHICS AND DEMOGRAPHICS IN DEMOCRACY

The Wild, Wild East

$\mathcal{A}$s a young boy growing up in Connecticut, it was always a tremendous thrill to come up to Maine for Christmas. It was like coming to the frontier. A trip to L. L. Bean was always included and in those days, that meant bumping into a Maine guide or a trapper, not just a bunch of people from New Jersey looking for women's blouses.

My cousin Charlie and his family lived in a house overlooking Baxter Boulevard in Portland and Christmas was always a magical time as we looked out over the bay and the twinkling lights of the city as the snow drifted down.

But the true high point of the trip to Portland at Christmas was the annual rat shoot always held on the day after Christmas. The location was always the same as well—Baxter Boulevard. We would go late in the afternoon just before dusk when the rats were the thickest.

Now for those of you familiar with today's Baxter Boulevard of yuppie fame, with its jogging paths and exercise stations and bird sanctuary, remember that there was a far different Baxter Boulevard in 1950. Then there were no yuppies, no joggers but many, many rats. Where the Cheverus playing fields are now were high grass, thick woods, and clay pits with pheasants and partridges and foxes.

And rats, hundreds and hundreds of them.

Open sewer pipes dumped into Back Bay and the marshes along the Boulevard had enough trash on it to make a very pleasant habitat for the rats. I can remember one Christmas counting over two hundred as we drove along shooting at them from the car with our BB guns.

Talk about excitement. My father would drive the car and my cousin and I would fire out the windows at the rats who, without a care in the world, were crawling all over the place. There was never a jogger or a walker in sight. It was a just an open shooting gallery, the personification of the Wild, Wild East to us.

I'm not sure we ever hit any rats in those early years, what with the speeding car and the moving rats and I'm sure we never killed any. In fact, most seemed hardly to notice us as we drove by.

But as we got to be nine or ten, we graduated from BB guns to .22s, and that Christmas, we knew we were really going to show the rats something out of Ernest Hemingway.

Now my father was a good sport about all this and he rather liked being the wheel man but I don't think he realized how different things would be that year with real guns. Once we began to blast real guns loudly out his car windows and it became pretty obvious that both other cars and some homes had people in them to hear and see this extravaganza, he got more and more nervous.

In our mania brought on by seeing rats dropping right and left, or spinning around and around with .22s through them, we kept firing even after he said, "We'd better stop now." We pretended that with the rush of air and the noise of the guns, we couldn't hear him.

But finally my father yelled out, "It's the cops" and sure enough, we saw a flashing blue light way over on what is now Tukey's bridge. Wow! I'm sure my father realized that the police car way over there wasn't responding to the two young desperadoes but we sure thought it was.

My father did a quick U-turn as we jerked in the guns and rolled up the windows. We sped off the boulevard and up into my cousin's driveway to hide the guns and ourselves from the cops.

Thankfully they never came, but that turned out to be the last of the Christmas car rat hunts. For years, my father told people about our close brush with the law and refused to take us any more. By the time we were old enough to drive ourselves, we were more interested in girls than rats.

But I never forgot the excitement of the Wild, Wild East of Maine at Christmas. Even after I grew up and became a Maine Guide myself, hunting all over Maine, I never lost the thrill of that early encounter.

There is, I think, more to this tale than a call for environmental clean up or a Maine childhood reminiscence too edgy for *Down East*, for it is this sense of wildness, of frontier, of Maine as the "Wild, Wild East" which remains such an intrinsic part of our Maine heritage—even though we all define that heritage differently.

For some of us, it's a canoe trip down the Allagash, or getting a moose permit, or going trout fishing, or seeing a bird we've never seen before way out in the woods. No matter how experienced, there remains about the Maine mystique a sense of the wild, even a sense of the frontier still with us at least in bits and pieces.

In 1987 we voted on a $35 million bond issue to purchase wild areas for all the people to enjoy. It passed overwhelmingly.

Since then, we've argued a lot about how wild the woods should be in two referenda about the Forest Compact and we've fought about bringing back wolves and access to the state's waterways and many other things affecting the way the open spaces of Maine are managed.

Through it all, we've had more in common than we realize. All of us want to keep a piece of Maine, at least in our mind's eye, a wild place. I have noticed over the years that while Maine people often differ as to what is the "right" wild experience—whether cutting down trees and shooting wolves or not cutting down trees and not shooting wolves—it is our personal mindscape of Maine which propels our sense of what we should be doing.

Almost every November, that clash of what is the essence of the Wild, Wild East is with us again as we are asked to debate a referendum on setting aside more Maine land for future generations and we will debate where that land should be and how it should be saved for future generations.

But at base, no matter how the election is framed, we will be debating about saving part of the Wild, Wild East, not just for ourselves but for our children and their children.

True in Any Light?

*M*aine has long been "on the frontier" and residual attitudes about hunting and a hunting culture persist, even in urban areas of the state. Yet, those who hunt find themselves under increasing pressure on many fronts.

In fact, sportsmen and women are beset on all sides with bad news: declining numbers, the encroachment of urban sprawl, blame for teenage shootings, and a host of other ills. And the patron saint of hunting, Ernest Hemingway, is under fierce attack as well.

His latest work, *True at First Light*, recently published posthumously by his son Patrick, has been savaged and trashed by reviewers from coast to coast. Seldom have I seen any work by a major writer so harshly received. Yet I doubt that any of the reviewers are hunters. Certainly none have ever hunted in Africa. One, from the *New York Times*, for example, has Hemingway killing a tiger in Africa, a most difficult feat unless he gunned one down in the Johannesburg zoo!

True at First Light is certainly not great literature but it is a loving portrait of what for the 1950s middle-aged white male author of declining prowess was the ideal safari. Simply put, Hemingway has created a parallel universe of virtual total wish fulfillment. Most hunting tales are an amalgam of reality and fantasy but this one is at the outer limits of the latter. In many ways, this work stands as the ultimate male hunting fantasy and shows, in stark relief, the inner Hemingway at his most endearingly adolescent.

The elements of fantasy in the safari are many:

First, it is of almost unbelievable length. Most hunting ventures are a week or two in length but this one is stupendous in duration. Indeed, when Hemingway picks up the narrative, it is already over three months long, with his wife Mary having been on a vision quest for a black maned lion for over ninety days!

Moreover in this dream safari, Hemingway is no longer just a hunting client. Although in real life, unlike Robert Rurak or James Mellon, Hemingway never really rose to the level of professional hunting greatness and was guided by others on most of his expeditions. In *True at First Light*, he has graduated to high and complete white hunter status, seemingly left on his own by his mentor, the legendary Philip Percival.[1]

As "Acting Temporary Game Ranger," he is in charge of the Kenyan district, guiding his own safari, warding off disease among the Africans, protecting his people from the Mau Mau insurgents, running a secret agent (The Informer), and showing one and all how to get the job done.

And what a shot he has become. When Miss Mary finally gets a chance at her lion, she manages to wound it in the foot and it is left to Bwana Hemingway to kill it at a great distance in the failing light. Later, Hemingway and a British ranger pace off the shot and agree never to tell the distance for it is too great and nobody would believe! You betcha!

There is also enough alcohol flowing for even the most ardent of Bud Light commercials. Pop pops a cold can at breakfast, carries around a flask of "wagini" with him all day, knocks back quarts of Tusker beer at lunch, and then really gets up a head of steam with whiskey as the sun is setting.

Never a hangover in this fantasy and not much about poor health habits either, although Miss Mary does ask somewhat diffidently that he not hit the beer at breakfast on the day they are finally going for the lion. After ninety-four days, she is rather keen on ending this lion quest without getting killed herself by Bwana Papa. Smart woman.

In real life, of course, Miss Mary knows of what she speaks for she once awoke in the middle of the Gulf Stream with the Papa-piloted boat going round and round in big circles, Papa Hemingway having passed out at the wheel about midnight.

In Hemingway's dream fantasy, the sex is pretty good too. In fact, it's damn good. Remember, this is pre-Viagra, so the sixty-plus year old Hemingway "making love" three times in one night, with his own wife, in the dark, on a small camp cot, without benefit of vibrators, erotic imagery, the Playboy Channel, or any other stimuli after a hard twelve hours of drinking belongs in the *Guinness Book of World Records* even before you throw in his earlier cavorting that day with the African lass Debba.

Debba, of course, belongs in every white hunter's fantasy. She is a young, nubile, compliant WaKamba girl completely smitten with our hero. She is lovely and proud and she adores Hemingway. She loves riding around in the Land Rover with him, her hand resting firmly on his pistol and carved leather holster.

She even loves smelling his salty sweat! (Note to Brett Favre: Real men don't use Right Guard on safari). He brings her father haunches of meat and wishes he could take her back to the United States as his second wife but there are laws about that sort of thing—although not out in the bush.

Whenever he is not finishing off one of Mary's wounded animals or being in charge of the district, he is buzzing around Debra, repeatedly kissing her on the head in public, and teaching her to communicate in—of all things—Spanish. Not chatting her up in KiKamba or English or Swahili as you might expect, but in Spanish.

When I read the Spanish dialogue, I was absolutely certain Hemingway was signaling us that *True Light* is a nearly perfectly self-contained fantasy—for whatever possible use could this poor girl have for Spanish in the Kenyan bush except to say "I love you" to him in this dream sequence?

There is also an additional, nearly miraculous plus for all white male hunters in their sixties—a totally understanding wife. Rather than getting upset about Hemingway's cavorting with Debba, Miss Mary says, "I like your fiancée very much because she is very much like me and I think she'd be a valuable extra wife if you need one." This is a level of male support almost beyond belief. Could Miss Mary be the early prototype for Hillary Rodham Clinton?

Perhaps best of all, this fantasy is never scheduled to end. Unlike most of Hemingway's books which have some sad or tragic ending to mar the revelry and enjoyment, *True at First Light* closes with

Hemingway planning to take the safari on the road after Christmas "to the Belgian Congo" and when Miss Mary asks Hem if they have enough "money" to keep the safari going, he allows as how they do.

So there you have it, fabulous shooting, on your own and in charge, lots of sex, no hangovers, no guilt, no worries about money, and an endless safari into the indefinite future.

A tad self-indulgent, you say, but then is that not something we've come to expect in our own age what with Barbara Streisand directing herself in *The Mirror Has Two Faces* or Robert Redford doing the same in *The Horse* (Will this film never end?) *Whisperer*.

But it's all in a good cause. In this age of feminism or is it now post-feminism—I'm never really sure—it is a rare thing to see the male psyche so exposed and vulnerable, yet oddly satisfied and at peace with itself, showing adolescent wish fulfillment writ large and unashamed. Men still need to know what it is they are truly missing even as the good old U.S. of A. women hold the World Cup.

For non-hunters, reading *True at First Light* can remind one of watching Frank Sinatra come out of retirement to sing. You know he'll never hit those notes again he used to and his pacing is going to be off, but there is something touching and poignant and affirming about listening to him try.

NOTE

1. Ernest Hemingway, *True at First Light* (New York: Scribner, 1999).

Up Ye Mighty Francos

$\mathcal{M}$aine's demographic makeup continues to affect the course of politics. Approximately 34 percent of the state's voting population self-identifies itself as of "English" descent, while 18 percent say they are Franco American and 15 percent say they are Irish American. Despite the electoral importance of the Franco Americans, they do not yet play a commensurate role in elected office for the major positions of governor, Congress, and U.S. Senate.

Within months after Governor Angus King's record-shattering performance in 1998, one which broke the previous three-way race record formerly held by Joshua Chamberlain in the election of 1868, various columnists and pundits began talking about who would succeed him in 2002.

In Maine politics, the governorship is the Holy Grail for the party faithful, much more important than either electing a senator or congressperson. So some, such as Speaker of the House Steve Rowe or Senate President Mark Lawrence or even State Senator Chellie Pingree may run against Senator Olympia Snowe next year in order to position themselves by getting statewide name recognition in a losing cause.

Even though political insiders are certain Congressman John Baldacci will run for the governorship and thus free up that congressional seat, there is lots of talk about other possible candidates as well.

For the Republicans, they are talking about a variety of people who could be formidable candidates such as Bill Haggett, Peter Mills,

Les Otten, Phil Harriman, Rick Bennett, Ross Connelly, and Jane Amero.

For the Democrats, John Baldacci is clearly the early front-runner but much of his ultimate success or failure will depend on where the former followers of Joe Brennan end up, especially in Maine's First Congressional District. Some Brennanistas have already decided that the Democratic nominee must be anybody but Baldacci.

In fact, so desperate are some Brennanistas to deny Baldacci the nomination that they are actually considering supporting Chellie Pingree despite her very liberal stances or even David Flanagan, the head of CMP. Can you imagine Flanagan carrying the Democratic banner?

Other non-Baldacci candidate possibilities mentioned from the constitutional office cohort include Treasurer Dale McCormick, Attorney General Drew Ketterer, and Secretary of State Dan Gwadowsky, but all seem supremely happy with their present situations and determined to stay there.

This seems both odd and even intolerable for didn't Democrats put them there in order for them to get some name recognition so they would run for higher office?

One Democratic legislator getting a lot of attention in southern Maine is Representative Tom Davidson of Brunswick, who is carving out an impressive career and gaining statewide recognition on many issues from consumer activism to electricity deregulation to environmental issues. Most importantly, he could probably raise ten times the money of other candidates.

But thus far, there are no Francos in the mix.

Where are the Franco American candidates in all the speculation about the gubernatorial race? Or for either of the two congressional races?

Why aren't people talking about Franco American candidates?

Since 1972, Francos have become the most important voting group in Maine, and their choices usually determine not only which candidates win statewide but which ballot measures pass and which fail as well.

Yet most Francos seem oblivious to their power.

Despite being 18 percent of the electorate and the most important ethnic group in the state in terms of determining the outcome of elections as the critical swing vote for both candidate and referenda elections, Francos rarely get the nominations for their party in major offices.

In fact, unless you count Margaret Chase Smith or Jim Longley as Francos, no Franco Americans have won major offices in Maine since World War II.

Where are the Francos in the speculation for governor in 2002?

Why has there been no public mention of the popular and ambitious Mayor of Lewiston, Kaileigh Tara, or Senator Georgette Barube, or Senator Mike Michaud of East Millinocket, head of the powerful Appropriations Committee, or former state senator from Waterville with very solid statewide support among sportsmen and sportswomen, Paul Jacques, or Senator Lloyd LaFountain III from Biddeford, or Representative Paul Tessier of Fairfield?

Why is no one talking about the dynamic senator from Frenchville, Judy Paradis (who will probably have to face former Speaker John Martin the next time around if she stays where she is)? She is a formidable candidate and politically astute.

Speaking of John Martin, who knows more about state government? Who could campaign smarter and harder? Who could unite Francos from Sanford to Westbrook to Ft. Kent? He'd give Baldacci a real run for his money. Why doesn't he lead the charge and become the champion of Francos?

Someone needs to step up and lead the Francos by example.

I think it is very important for Francos to recognize the power they already have and the greater power they could have if they united.

We need Franco candidates for the major offices.

At this point, I'd take a candidate for congress or governor with even half a Franco heritage, someone like highly respected and intelligent former state senator and Auburn mayor John Cleveland whose mother was a Chabot, or successful businessman Mike Fiori whose mother was a Pelletier.

Come to think of it, "Governor Mike Pelletier Fiori" does have an interesting ring to it and his administration would be quite a team effort.

His wife, Maine Bureau of Health Chief Dora Ann Mills, just won a tremendous victory in getting smoking banned in all restaurants across Maine and sending tobacco's premier lobbying firm scurrying for cover, driving one of its partners to the Holy Land for rest and recovery. She is a former Democratic National Committee woman and a skillful political figure who is very achievement oriented.

I believe the cities of Auburn and Lewiston should host a Pan-Franco meeting in the near future, bringing together the leading Franco American figures, political, social, cultural, and economic, from Sanford, Biddeford, Westbrook, Saco, Brunswick, Auburn, Waterville, and the Saint John Valley to explore uniting the Franco American communities of Maine behind strong and vigorous Franco candidates for governor and for Congress in 2002 when both the governorship and the Baldacci congressional seat will become vacant.

Up ye mighty Francos.

It's time.

Changing Voting Demographics

$\mathcal{A}$s some of these essays indicate, political actors can play important roles in shaping not only electoral outcomes but also long term political trends. We tend to focus on these interesting and dynamic personalities. But many electoral shifts happen beyond the horizon of most Mainers and many elections are decided against the backdrop of deeper and longer-term shifts in the body politic.

One of the reasons it is so much fun being a professor and a columnist is that you are always challenged to deal with new data and to put it in the proper historical context. Many people called, wrote, and sent e-mails about the Francos and asked for follow-up analysis.

To review, I have often made the point of how important are the Franco Americans to elections in Maine. They are the premier swing vote and have determined the outcome of most of the close candidate races and ballot measures in Maine especially since 1972 and the elimination of the "big box" (or straight party ticket) voting. Franco Americans have elected such diverse people as Bill Cohen, Jim Longley Sr., Dave Emery, Olympia Snowe, and Angus King to name but the most prominent.

For me, an appreciation of the Franco American role has not been simply an academic enterprise to be taught to students, it has had a real world grounding and payoff.

Ever since I was the campaign manager for Bill Cohen in 1972 when he first ran for Congress, I have been fascinated by the Franco American voter in Maine. In 1972, fully two-thirds of all Franco Americans were registered Democrats and most voted a straight Democratic ticket. The Franco American strongholds such as Biddeford/Saco, Lewiston/Auburn, and the St. John's Valley brought in huge majorities for Democratic candidates.

But from my earliest polling, I always noted that while the Francos were registered Democrat and usually voted that way, many of them shared "Republican" values such as distrust of government, emphasis on small business concerns, and exhibited a pattern of seeing the government as often the problem as the solution.

This compared with a much different profile for the other pillar of the Democratic Party in Maine, the Irish Americans. Over half of them were registered Democrats as well but they had a far different psychographic profile. Irish Americans more often saw government as a solution not a problem, welcomed expanded government employment, and were far less likely than their Franco compatriots to be sympathetic to the needs of small business.

I believed then, as I do now, that the key to any Republican and Independent success in Maine depends on appealing to the Franco American swing vote (18 percent plus statewide) for even a near split in the voting pattern means that the Democrat cannot win no matter what else they do if that key element is lost.

Why did the Franco Americans end up being such a swing vote in Maine's elections?

I think I know why. When the second wave of French immigrants came down from Quebec after the American Civil War (the first wave came earlier from Atlantic Canada and settled in the St. John's Valley), they found work in the shoe and textile factories and paper mills of Biddeford, Saco, Sanford, Westbrook, Lewiston, Auburn, Brunswick, Waterville, and Winslow. Many of their basic societal and governmental values should have made them Republicans but for the fact that the mill owners were already Republicans. That coupled with discrimination against them as well as the Irish and other minority groups by the descendents of the English settlers made the Democratic Party a more natural fit for them for the first one hundred years they were in Maine.

Francos were overwhelmingly Democratic and could be counted on to vote that way from the time of their enfranchisement until 1972. Part of it was habit; they were Democrat and voted that way. Part of it was institutional; there was a big box at the top of the ballot which enabled anyone who wished to vote a straight ticket. Many Franco Americans did so. Finally, part of the ongoing Democratic success among Francos was also the result of a self-fulfilling prophecy: Republican candidates "knew" that the Franco Americans were going to vote Democrat so they didn't bother to campaign among them very much or to find out what they wanted.

All this changed in 1972. Thanks largely to the efforts of Bob Monks, who led the fight to eliminate the "big box" (which occurred by the time of the general elections in November 1972), Franco Americans theoretically came "into play."

They actually came into play when Bill Cohen campaigned extensively in the Franco American communities and walked across Maine. From a working-class background (his father was a baker who got up at 2 AM every morning to bake the bread and rolls), Cohen not only projected an image different from that of previous Republican candidates, he also spent enough time in and among the Franco communities so that they could appreciate how many values he and they shared.

Cohen was elected in 1972 precisely because the Franco American vote split significantly. For example, normally the Republican candidate came out of Androscoggin County down 23,000 votes but in 1972, Cohen lost the Androscoggin valley by only 6,000 votes. His small business orientation, his blue-collar background, and his basic distrust of government for all political solutions all resonated with Franco Americans. In subsequent elections, he carried Lewiston, Auburn, and the Androscoggin valley on his way to eight straight elections without a loss.

The profile of Franco American voters has shifted rather continuously from that time. In order to check on the extent of this shift, I recently asked Dave Emery of Scientific Marketing to run an analysis of the standard voting blocs of Maine politics, the English, the Irish, and the Franco Americans and cross tabulate them against party enrollments. Emery currently has the best data bank in Maine when it comes to operational polling results and parameters.

What follows is his assessment based on 2,100 interviews and has a margin of error of plus or minus 2 percent at the 99th level of confidence. Bear in mind also that these are real voters who have self-identified themselves as to which ethnic heritage they choose for themselves.

Currently in Maine, there are 29 percent Republicans, 32 percent Democrats and 39 percent Independents registered to vote. Of all registered voters, 35–36 percent are of English or British heritage (self-defined), 18–19 percent are of Franco heritage, and 13–14 percent are of Irish heritage.

The Franco Americans remain the most important swing group, but their party affiliation has changed dramatically. Thirty years ago, approximately two-thirds of Francos were Democrats. Today, that number is down substantially to 45 percent. Twenty-two percent of Francos self-identify themselves as Republicans (up from about 12 percent earlier) and 33 percent are Independent (a number just about double what it once was).

So the Francos have not only become more independent behaviorally, i.e., how they vote, they have also become more "Independent" in terms of their actual registration. This represents a sea change in Maine politics.

The Republicans have lost some of their English cohorts to the Democrats (think of the suburban belt around Portland with upscale Democratic voters) and to Independents (think of the rural vote for Ross Perot in the 2nd District).

The Irish too have moved, with 25 percent of them registered as Republicans, 37 percent as Democrats, and 37 percent as Independents.

This means that the Francos are not only still the most important swing voting group both demographically and psychographically (lifestyle and value orientation), they are now essential to Republican success in general elections but also twice as important in statewide Republican primaries as they were when Bill Cohen first ran for office.

The Franco Americans have the power to determine who will be the next senator, governor, or representative.

Turnout

$\mathcal{M}$aine lost. And I was happy. It doesn't usually work that way. I like it when Maine wins—especially with regard to voter turnout. Usually Maine leads the nation in voter participation and that gives me a sense of pride that we have shown the nation that democracy is alive and well in the Pine Tree state.

But not this time. This time Maine finished second to Minnesota in the voter turnout results for the November 2000 elections. 67.3 percent of Mainers turned out to vote compared with 68.75 percent of those from Minnesota and Governor King graciously sent off some lobsters to Jesse Ventura to pay off an "unofficial" bet. Nationwide the turnout was 53.7 percent.

However, there was much more to the story because voter turnout played a vital role in the outcome of two different ballot measures. As I have stressed before, turnout usually doesn't make any difference in well-run ballot measure campaigns. You can win if 80 percent of the people vote or 18 percent of the people vote.

But, there are exceptions that prove the rule and Maine saw a couple of them this election cycle and both are worth noting. Sometimes, the margin of outcome depends on election turnout and people's perceptions of them.

For example, advocates for gay rights believed—erroneously as it turned out—that turnout *qua* turnout would help their cause. They assumed that the major reason they lost Gay Rights II in February 1998 was that only 17 percent of the electorate had voted and if over 60 percent had voted they would have won.

Unfortunately for someone like myself who wanted the gay rights bill to pass, this error was compounded by two others, including believing wildly inflated polling numbers put out by some state newspapers (but not the *Sun Journal!*), and not conveying a sense of urgency that there was a problem in Maine and that it needed to be addressed now and by this measure.

But the most interesting connection between turnout and outcome had to do with Question 1, the measure to legalize physician-assisted suicide. As the campaign progressed, the polling data began to diverge substantially from the tracking on Questions 2 (The Forestry Referendum) and 3 (Casino Gambling).

In both the forestry and gambling campaigns, there soon developed parallel if slightly different patterns. Even with several weeks to go until Election Day, most likely voters—those voters "guaranteed" to show up on Election Day—became opposed to both measures in very high numbers with six out of ten Maine voters turning thumbs down on both issues. Less likely voters—those who say they are going to vote but normally don't—tracked the same. Note, we are speaking here of the people who vote as opposed to unregistered voters and a third category of registered voters: those who never vote. Somewhat unkindly but accurately, these are referred to in campaign argot as "garbage voters" since they are worthless to pollsters and practitioners alike even though you have to identify them in order to determine who is actually going to vote.

In our real life examples, the opponents of Question 3 were not able to run a closing commercial and thus the less likely voters ended up voting like most likely voters and the measure was defeated by a 6–4 margin. Opponents of Question 2, however, ran an extremely effective "closer" commercial and impacted all voters even more, picking up approximately 8 percent in the last five or six days to win by a 7–3 margin. Incredibly enough, the No vote, which had been behind by 2–1 when the campaign started, ended up carrying virtually *every* town in Maine. And that includes the People's Republic of Arrowsic with a 56.5 percent No tally!

These patterns were not mirrored in the vote on Assisted Suicide however. Although initial polling figures showed 72 percent of Maine people in favor of the concept, as health care professionals and others began to point out the flaws in the proposed legislation, opposition grew and support waned. But this did not happen in the same way as in the other elections in terms of turnout. It soon became clear that for Question 1, turnout would be very significant.

David Emery and his firm, Scientific Marketing, did the daily tracking for the Coalition Against the Dangers of Physician-Assisted Suicide and picked up a very unusual correlation between voting patterns and turnout patterns.

With one week to go, most likely voters had changed their minds significantly and those voting "No" had a discernible lead of 8 percent. In other words, if only the more or less 60 percent of the voting population which self-identified themselves as "guaranteed" to vote showed up on Election Day voted, the measure would have been defeated 55 percent to 45 percent.

But unlike the situation in Questions 2 and 3, the more voters who showed up to vote, the closer would be the vote. In fact, less likely voters actually favored the measure. Thus, turnout on Election Day would go a long way to determining the outcome. This issue would become what is called in politics "turnout driven." The closer to a 70 percent turnout, the better for the Yes side and the closer to a 60 percent turnout, the better for the No side.

Dave Emery's prediction based on the final tracking cut proved to be incredibly accurate and is well worth noting here. On the eve of the election, he stated "I am very confident of a 'No' victory. The margin, however, depends significantly on turnout. At 580,000, the margin will be 9 percent, at 620,000 it will be 5 percent, at 640,000 it will be 3 percent, and at 660,000 it will be 1 percent."

Emery had correctly seen the sophisticated and subtle correlation between turnout and voting patterns on this issue and hit the prediction right on the head. Exit polling on Election Day (conducted very ably by Mal Leary of Maine Public Radio) as well as election night returns underscored the validity of Emery's assessment.

In Maine, 67.34 percent or 647,311 voters went to the polls and Question 1 failed by less than 2 percent, a margin of 17,000. In the world of often-inflated polling claims, it is worth remembering the old Maine saying that "even a broken clock is right twice a day." In other words, even bad polling can capture truly wide spreads in voter sentiment. Closer elections, however, challenge many polling concerns as witness the many mistaken projections on the Gay Rights initiative.

In the case of Assisted Suicide, however, to get such accurate results when there are so many impediments to assessing linkage between turnout and voting patterns in real-life, real-time elections was truly remarkable.

"This was a particularly difficult call to make," said Emery. "The pattern was hard to spot because towns with apparent demographic similarities voted differently. Without day-to-day tracking reports, I never would have caught it."

In the election cycle of 2000, Dave Emery was on top of his game and showed the profession how prediction can and should be done. Plus he got his deer this fall. A man for all seasons!

One Delight More: The Delight of Teaching

*A*s much as I love politics—and I love politics passionately—I love teaching more. There is something stimulating, richly rewarding, and always challenging about the interplay of ideas, concepts, backgrounds, and styles that brings teachers, students, and subjects together.

I currently teach a course in Maine politics, which meets at 8:30 AM. I routinely wake up at 5 or 5:30 AM, too excited to sleep any longer, as giddy as Scrooge on Christmas Day. I am truly exhilarated about what I am going to say in class that day. I can't wait to see how the students are going to respond and what they are going to contribute to the ongoing quest for knowledge.

I have been very fortunate over the years to have taught at a number of schools: Tufts, Dartmouth, Vassar, The College of the Virgin Islands, the University of Southern Maine, and, of course, my beloved Bowdoin. At each and every one, I encountered students who had a thirst for learning, who wanted to immerse themselves in subjects about which they knew little or nothing. The interplay with those students, stimulating their minds and being stimulated in return, has been one of the great joys of my life.

My own journey in learning has been a fortunate one. I was the first person in my extended family to attend college. From the beginning, I felt the burden of having to succeed, not just for myself but for others. At the same time, I saw learning as an opportunity, a path of upward mobility.

My father, a carpenter and builder, worked very long hours for most of his life, stopping active work only when he was in his early 80s.

185

Those who write of the dignity of honest toil are only half correct. There is also a significant and never-ending stress of dependency, of having to try to please those who have the economic power over you.

For her part, my mother always stressed how education was a pathway to freedom, a way to escape that grinding dependency, and an opportunity to gain economic, social, and personal altitude. I ended up at Bowdoin College in 1958 by a set of fortuitous events. One of our neighbors in Hartford, Connecticut, where we lived until I was ten, was Stan Fish, principal of one of the local schools. When I was in high school, he invited me to a Bowdoin Club meeting and told me I should apply. Then, when I visited Bowdoin it snowed and the campus seemed truly magical.

Most important of all for someone with a working class background, the Director of Admissions, Hubie Shaw, got up from his chair during my interview, came around the desk and shook my hand saying, "What will it take Chris, to reduce your applications to just this one?" I told him of my need for financial assistance. "Done," he said and my life was inexorably transformed for I never could have afforded a Bowdoin education with just our family resources.

Ironically enough, when I first came to Bowdoin that fall, I was truly miserable. In fact, I was the most miserable I've ever been in my life. I came from a big urban high school with a couple of thousand students, lots of diversity, and lots of girls.

Bowdoin was not only much harder than New London High School, it was, in those days, the oddest combination of a monastery and periodic bacchanalia. In addition, my parents had instilled in me a career goal that quickly became an impossible burden. I was to become a doctor. I was premed.

I was miserable. From the first time I walked into the biology lab, I wanted to throw up.

It took me the entire first semester to extricate myself from my homesickness, my misguided career path, and the overwhelming anxiety of a self-imposed workload. I was so afraid of failing and letting my family down that I studied eighty hours a week and it was not unusual for me that first semester to run back to my room from my class which ended at 12:30 and study for fifteen minutes before lunch was served at 12:45!

It took me until the second semester to figure out this was no way to live. But studying eighty hours a week that first semester put a lot of other things in my life into perspective.

I never thought much about being a teacher until my junior year. It was only after I'd discarded being a doctor or lawyer that I even thought about it. Again, it was a single individual who changed my life. The Dean of the College (and the students, and the faculty) was Nat Kendrick, who taught modern European history. He had been responsible for my getting an increased scholarship when my father was stricken with a cerebral spasm and unable to work for six months. Now he asked if I would like to give a lecture in his class.

The talk was a major revelation.

While the class consisted of my peers and some seniors, I nevertheless felt at home lecturing to them. I knew I had more knowledge about the battle of Lepanto Gulf than they did. Hell, they'd never heard of that battle which I saw as a major turning point in the history of West War. It was a thrill to stand there in class and watch people write down what you said. Now, of course, I know that many times people are not writing down what you say in class but making to-do notes, shopping lists, and doodling. But at the time I thought they were writing down exactly what I said.

Later, the Dean had a question on the hour exam about the lecture and that seemed very rewarding to have someone graded on their knowledge of what you said. The next semester, the Dean asked me to give another lecture and this time I chose the battle of Stalingrad, then (1957), virtually unknown to Americans. I had my cousin Charles Petersen to thank for stimulating my interest in World War II and his in-depth knowledge of the subject was an inspiration to me. He later earned his Ph.D. in military history and for many years taught that subject.

Those two lectures—and the chance to deliver them—changed my life and I have always encouraged my own students to give oral reports in class and in special situations, allowed some to become teaching assistants and give their own lectures in my class. As professors, we all like to think we lead by example, but sometimes we truly lead when we provide opportunities.

When I was in graduate school at the Fletcher School of Law and Diplomacy, I flirted with going into the State Department and the CIA and was accepted into both. But being a professor won out and I have always been happy with my career choice and grateful for those along the way who made it possible for me to pursue my career.

Teaching about politics is doubly rewarding. First, there is the joy of teaching itself, the constant stimulation to learn more about your subject and to stay ahead of—or at least not too far behind—the knowledge curve. During summers and vacations, I am always writing new lectures and rewriting old ones as I learn more about the great process of politics.

Second, there is the stability and peace of the classroom, a sanctuary from modern life where it is possible, if only for an hour and a half, to turn down the volume and the rhetoric and have an engaging time of stimulating tranquility. It is that combination of stimulation and tranquility that is so appealing about teaching. In the ivory tower, you are insulated from many of the pressures of the world, daily life, and some destructive forms of competition.

Third, there is the constant simulation of new students each and every September. Although September is the end of summer and the end of one growing cycle, in the classroom, it is always springtime and the beginning of another growing cycle. Every September brings new students from new places with new backgrounds and a never-ending challenge to make things relevant. The mere passage of time, as well as the generational process, means that you have constantly to update your examples, contexts, lessons and continually challenge their relevance.

Fourth, there is the intertwined nature of speaking and writing. I am fortunate to be in a field where what you say is what you can write and what you write is what you can say in class. My lectures are written with an eye toward history and being recorded somewhere. Because of that, I believe I am more careful about the conclusions I dish out in class. Conversely, the stimulation and challenge of the classroom make my lectures clearer and most relevant as they turn into chapters in books. That interplay between the spoken word, the refined lecture, and the printed article or chapter is both professionally enriching and a constant source of dynamism.

Finally, there is the joy of seeing students carry on, if not your work, at least using the tools you provided. It is always enjoyable, of course, if they follow you in your causes, but it is equally satisfying if they show they have learned from you—even if this takes the form of using your insights and techniques to pursue opposite goals and promote different causes.

Teaching is more than a delight. It is a blessing.

It is a blessing for which I am very grateful.

Index

abortion: Birth or Late Term Abortion Ban referendum, 49–53; Maine as pro-Choice or pro-Life, 143–46
Abramson, Joel, 10
Adams, Mary, 10
Ad Media, 57, 58, 90
advertisements, TV. *See* commercials
Africa, author's experience in, 32
African Americans: at Dartmouth College, 32–33; dragging death of African American man, 31–32; leadership, 33; and partisan voting, 31–32, 33–34; sentiments toward Republican Party, 31
Allen, Ken, 148
Allen, Thomas (Tom), 85, 120, 143
The American Voter (Campbell, Converse, et. al.), 45
Amero, Jane, 85, 86
Ames, Patty, 5
Andrews, Thomas (Tom), 17–18, 120
armed forces. *See* military
arms. *See* gun control; weapons acquisitions/development
Aroostok County, 18
arrogance, fable about, 131–34

Bailey, John, 46
Bailey Kennelly, Barbara, 48
Baldacci, John: abortion issue, 143; running for governor, 137–41, 173, 174
ballots: "big box" on, 178–79; getting on, 11; and polling, 85
Bangor Daily News (newspaper), 50, 55, 56
Barube, Georgette, 10, 175
Baxter Boulevard, 165–66
beliefs, political, 72–74
Beliveau, Severin, 140
Bennett, Richard (Rick), 174
Biafra, Jellow, 126
"big box", on voting ballots, 178–79
Birth or Late Term Abortion Ban referendum, 49
blacks. *See* African Americans
Blixen, Karen, 147
Bowdoin College (Maine): and author's decision to teach politics, 186–88; author and Bill Cohen at, 71; professor's involvement in political commercial, 57–58
Bradford, Peter, 92

189

Franco Americans: as candidates, 173–76; as voters, 177–80
freedom: price of, 28; of speech, 50–53
Fruen, Jeanette, 49
Fuentes, Maria, 5, 10
fun, politics as, 71

gambling casinos, 153–56
The Gannett Corporation, 53
Gaskin, Stephen, 126
gay rights: Gay Rights I amendment, 3; general discussion, 157–61; and voter turnout, 181–82
"Gay Rights III." (column in *Sun Journal*), 3
Glenn, John, 60
Goldthweight, Jill, 2
Gore, Albert Jr. (Al): kissing incident, 97–100; smirk of, 98–99. *See also* presidential election, of 2000
Gore, Tipper, 97–100
gratitude, of author to friends/military, 59–62
Green Party: official platform, 126; Ralph Nader running under, 125–30
Greenspan, Alan, 114–15, 117
Greenwood, Raymond, 95–97, 99
Guerin, Kathy, 57
Gulf War, 23
gun control: and hunting, 147–48; John Baldacci on, 139; Maine Legislature on, 83–84
Gwadowsky, Daniel (Dan), 174

Haggett, William (Bill), 173
Hardy, Jay, 105
Harrimany, Phillip (Phil), 174
Harron family, 53

Hart, Gary, 60
Hathaway, William (Bill), 143
Havey, Jack, 57–58, 90
Heath, Michael (Mike), 50
Heath, Mike, 64
hegemonic United States, 23–24, 26, 28
Hemingway, Ernest, 169–72
Hennessey, Thomas (Tom), 148
Higgins, Jay, 50
hiking, access to land for, 148–51
Hitler, Adolph, 23
homosexuals. *See* gay rights
Horan, Judy, 51
hunting: access to land for, 148–51; and gun control, 147–48; Hemingway's *True at First Light*, 169–72
Huntley, Lievy, 153–55
Hussein, Saddam, 23
Hydro Quebec, 92

incumbents, campaigning against, 77–81
Indian gambling casinos, 153–56
informed ballots, 85
An Insider's Guide to Maine Politics (Potholm), 9
Irish Americans, as voters, 178
"Issues and Inheritance in the Formation of Party Identification" (article), 47–48
Ivins, Molly, 128

Jackson, Jessie, 13
Jacques, Paul, 148, 175
Jalkut, Dick, 92
Jennings, M. Kent, 47–48
Johnson, Beryl-Ann, 57, 90
Johnson, Greg (Grog), 60–61
Kagan, Donald, 23
Kaufman, David (Dave), 51–52

United Soviet Socialists Republic
(USSR), Reagan's effect on,
116–17
United States. *See* defense-related
issues
USA Today (newspaper), 99
USS Kennedy (ship), 4th of July
festivities on, 59–61
USSR (United Soviet Socialists
Republic), Reagan's effect on,
116–17

Vafiades, Lew, 56
Vanderweide, Harold (Harry), 148
Vietnam War, 22–23, 28
Vigue, Peter, 140
voting: abortion issue, 143–46;
African Americans votes, 31–32,
33–34; demographics, 177–80; by
Franco Americans, 177–80; by
Irish Americans, 178; partisan,
31–32, 33–34; two votes instead
of one, 42–43. *See also*
presidential election, of 2000;
turnout, voter

Walden (Thoreau), 3–4
Wallace, George, 32
Wall Street Journal (newspaper), 99

war: as continuation of politics,
18–19; position of Western world
toward, 24; power to get out of
hand, 19; preparedness for,
20–24, 28; and willpower, 36. *See
also* defense-related issues
Washington Post (newspaper), 61
WCSH (Channel 6 TV station), 51,
81
weapons acquisitions/development:
amount of, 25–26, 27–28;
disarmament, 21; process, 19–20.
See also defense-related issues
WGME (Channel TV station), 51
wilderness: access to, 148–51;
conservation of, 148–51
Wilson, Woodrow, 19
WLBZ (Channel 2 TV station), 51
WMTV (Channel 8 TV station),
51–52
worker's compensation reforms,
140
World Trade Center attack, 35–37
World War II, disarmament
following, 21
WPXI (Channel 51 TV station), 51
writing, political, 4, 188

Young, Christine, 52

Other Cooper Square Press Titles of Interest

ROE V. WADE
The Untold Story of the Landmark
Supreme Court Decision That
Made Abortion Legal
Updated Edition
Marian Faux
404 pp., 15 b/w photos
0-8154-1093-X
$19.95

MEMOIR
My Life and Themes
Conor Cruise O'Brien
464 pp., 27 b/w photos
0-8154-1064-6
$30.00 (cloth)

THOMAS JEFFERSON
Passionate Pilgrim
Alf J. Mapp Jr.
446 pp., 16 pages of b/w illustrations
1-56833-020-0
$16.95

THE JEFFERSON SCANDALS
A Rebuttal
Virginius Dabney
170 pp., 18 b/w illustrations
0-8191-7821-7
$14.95

RUSSELL KIRK
A Critical Biography of a
Conservative Mind
James E. Person, Jr.
280 pp., 20 b/w photos
1-56833-131-2
$26.95 (cloth)

THE COMPLETE BOLIVIAN
DIARIES OF CHÉ GUEVARA &
Other Captured Documents
Edited with an introduction by
Daniel James
New introduction by
Henry Butterfield Ryan
384 pp., 50 illustrations, 2 maps
0-8154-1056-5
$18.95